'Here is a much-needed b[
racism, injustice, poverty, [
for contemplation. We need to hear it – there is much here that
applies to our world today.'
Esther de Waal, writer and scholar

'I do appreciate Ian Cowley's interleaving of storytelling with
spiritual reflection. It is good to have the story of UCM told to a
wider audience than South Africa.

Ian's tribute to Steve Biko is welcome and true, and so is his
account of white students' struggle on the matter of conscription.

His major concern with contemplation fits well into his account
of this crucial time in the South African church struggle.'
**John Davies, former bishop of Shrewsbury and one-time national chaplain
of the Anglican Students' Federation of South Africa**

'What an incredible book this is! I was deeply moved reading
it. It is very inspiring and ignited a hope that we can be agents
of change in this world. As someone who has known the value
of contemplative prayer and practice in my own life, it felt like
a gentle call back to that which I know and love, without being
remotely judgemental. In fact, the whole book brings a wonderful
balance of challenge without condemnation.

I pray that all who read this book will examine afresh their
response to the issues raised and explore the riches of contemplative prayer for themselves.'
Louise Rose, community projects manager, Fresh Hope Ministry, Stamford

'*The Contemplative Struggle* is a generous gift and a profound
challenge. Ian Cowley draws on a deep well of (sometimes painful)
personal experience to pour out this vision of contemplation
in action. If you're tired of rootless activism and otherworldly
spirituality, and you're looking for the common ground where
prayer and protest can flourish, you need to read this book.'
**Chris Webb, deputy warden of Launde Abbey
and author of *God Soaked Life***

The Bible Reading Fellowship
15 The Chambers, Vineyard
Abingdon OX14 3FE
brf.org.uk

The Bible Reading Fellowship (BRF) is a Registered Charity (233280)

ISBN 978 0 85746 982 3
First published 2021
10 9 8 7 6 5 4 3 2 1 0
All rights reserved

Acknowledgements
Unless otherwise acknowledged, scripture quotations are taken from The New
Revised Standard Version of the Bible, Anglicised edition, copyright © 1989, 1995
by the Division of Christian Education of the National Council of the Churches of
Christ in the United States of America. Used by permission. All rights reserved.

Scripture quotations marked NKJV are taken from the New King James Version®.
Copyright © 1982 by Thomas Nelson. Used by permission. All rights reserved.

A catalogue record for this book is available from the British Library

Printed and bound by CPI Group (UK) Ltd, Croydon CR0 4YY

God is our refuge and strength, a very present help in trouble.
Therefore we will not fear, though the earth should change,
though the mountains shake in the heart of the sea...
'Be still, and know that I am God!'
PSALM 46:1–2, 10

He prayeth best, who loveth best.
Samuel Taylor Coleridge, 'The Rime of the Ancient Mariner'

The
Contemplative
Struggle

Radical discipleship
in a broken world

A South African journey

Ian Cowley

Acknowledgements

It has taken a long time for me to be able to write this book. The experience of being a member of the University Christian Movement in South Africa in the early 1970s changed my life. But it was also deeply painful, and it is only now that I am able to speak and write about some of the things that happened then.

At the Thomas Merton Society conference in 2018, Stephen Dunhill pointed me to the two main themes in the life and writings of Thomas Merton: 'contemplation' and 'struggle'. Later that year I spent a day with my friend Steve Hobbs reflecting on our experience as white South African Christians who were formed in our discipleship in the context of the South African situation in the 1970s and 1980s. The idea of writing this book and bringing together these two key strands of our Christian experience began to come together.

I discussed these ideas with Olivia Warburton from BRF at the New Wine conference in 2019, and she encouraged me to put together a proposal for this book. I am enormously grateful to Olivia for her belief in this project and her unfailing support. Dan Och at BRF has been excellent in the editing and production of the book.

There are so many people that I would like to be able to thank. I think, for example, of Peter Johnstone, who first drew me into UCM when I was only 17 years old. There have been many others along the way. But they are simply too numerous to mention by name.

I am very grateful to those who have helped me with their wisdom and advice, in particular Andrew Judge, Richard Cook, Steve Pearson, Philip Dale, Pat Dale and Len Abrams. I also thank Bill Houston, John Davies, Trish Baker, Christopher Forsyth and Louise Rose. Diane Faux worked alongside me in typing and word-processing the manuscript, and was an invaluable help and encouragement.

Thank you also to Alison, who has taught me more about the meaning of love than anyone else.

Above all, thanks be to God, who has called me and has been faithful and merciful, over and over again.

List of abbreviations

ANC	African National Congress
ASF	Anglican Students' Federation
CAP	Christians Against Poverty
NCFS	National Catholic Federation of Students
NUSAS	National Union of South African Students
SASO	South African Students' Organisation
SCA	Students' Christian Association
SHEP	Stamford Household Essentials Project
SRC	Students' Representative Council
UCM	University Christian Movement

Contents

Introduction

Beginning in the late 1960s and through the early 1970s, leading up to the Soweto riots of 1976 and the subsequent clampdown by the state, something remarkable took place in South Africa. A broad base of interlinked progressive activists came together and radically transformed the internal struggle against apartheid. At the heart of this movement were Steve Biko and the Black Consciousness Movement, church leaders and ministers, student activists and university teachers and academics, black and white. By 1978 the very foundation of the internal opposition to apartheid had changed. Now there could be no turning back the clock, no matter how many people were detained or murdered by the state. I was privileged to arrive as a young undergraduate at the University of Natal in February 1969. I lived through those years and was directly involved in much of the student activism of that time.

What happened to me changed my life and the lives of many of my closest friends. We were part of an extraordinary period of history, which indelibly changed South Africa.

It has taken me many years to work through and reflect properly upon the events of that time. At the heart of all this were two key vocations. First, there was a dawning sense of the power of the love of God in Jesus Christ and the hope which this gives to a broken world. Second, I became utterly convinced of the imperative to live and work in whatever way I could to bring about a better, more just and more compassionate world. This vision of life and vocation has guided me and held me firm from those days until now.

I met Steve Biko at a University Christian Movement (UCM) formation school at Redacres, near Pietermaritzburg, in September 1969. This was probably one of the last UCM events that Steve attended. He was a student at the University of Natal Medical School in Durban and had been active in the multiracial National Union of South African Students (NUSAS) during 1966 and 1967. At the 1968 UCM conference at Stutterheim, Steve Biko and a group of black delegates agreed to set up a new black-led student organisation which would be able to properly understand and advance black aspirations. This led to the founding in 1969 of the South African Students' Organisation (SASO) and the emergence in South Africa of Black Theology and the Black Consciousness Movement. This movement has had an inestimable impact on the history of South Africa and the liberation of South Africa from the evil of apartheid. It also has much to teach us in the contemporary struggle against racism and inequality.

Steve Biko was a man of extraordinary ability, intellect and charisma, surely one of the greatest leaders that South Africa has ever produced. He died on 12 September 1977 after suffering dreadful torture and cruelty and lying on the floor of a police van for 12 hours while being driven from Port Elizabeth to Pretoria. When I heard that Steve had been killed, I was profoundly shocked. I still struggle to comprehend the enormity of the loss of his death. From that moment something in me shattered, and I don't think it will ever be mended. Whatever naive sense I had that the white South African government might be amenable to gradual change disappeared forever on that day.

Steve Biko saw with great clarity the need to directly confront racism, injustice and poverty. He also saw that black people in South Africa were not powerless to bring about change. None of us is powerless. We all have to start rediscovering our own God-given dignity and humanity and our freedom in Christ. We truly discover our vocation in life when we choose to live for the purpose for which God created us and to become the person, and people, that he has intended us to be.

Black consciousness articulated the need for black people to step away from the white liberals in the churches and universities in order to be themselves and to be able to speak freely. They saw 'white

liberals' as people with a sense of guilt or shame over their privileged position but who nonetheless continued to exercise power and
control. Barney Pityana, a close friend and colleague of Steve Biko,
describes one young white person saying, 'I am so pleased I am no
longer a white liberal. I am a radical now.'[1] Pityana says that many
young whites who were influenced by Steve Biko were later 'to be
found within the trade unions and in legal-aid work or have become
academics who use their learning to advance the cause of liberation'.[2]
Some of us also became priests and ministers of the church, as did
Pityana and other black consciousness leaders.

Jesus Christ is the true radical. My experience of meeting with black
students at UCM and the Anglican Students' Federation (ASF) gatherings enabled me to hear for myself the pain and the oppression of
black people in South Africa. This led me directly to the call to follow
Jesus Christ in radical discipleship.

The word 'radical' derives from the Latin *radix*, meaning 'root'. To
be radical means to go to the root of things and to address the root
issues that affect everything else. John the Baptist proclaimed, 'Even
now the axe is lying at the root of the trees; every tree therefore that
does not bear good fruit is cut down and thrown in the fire' (Luke 3:9).
Ronald Sider writes:

> Radical discipleship means nothing more – and nothing less –
> than practising what we preach. It means living out the concrete
> implications of our most basic Christian confession: Jesus of
> Nazareth is truly Immanuel, God with us. It means surrender-
> ing every area of our lives – our security, our economics, even
> our politics – to the sovereign, unconditional Lordship of the
> Incarnate One who came and lived among us as the carpenter
> from Nazareth.[3]

What I quickly discovered was that radical discipleship means always
being to some degree out of step with institutional religion and its
power structures. In South Africa, the temptation for white Christians

was to escape into prayer and conventional religion when we ought to have been facing issues and taking action.

If we recognise Jesus as 'the way, and the truth, and the life' (John 14:6), we acknowledge him as the source of all truth, righteousness and holiness. To live in the truth is to live as Jesus lived. To know Jesus and to follow him is to be changed into his likeness. This inner transformation leads directly to outward obedience and action. The two must go together. Both spirituality and activism are essential and indispensable components of true Christian discipleship.

In South Africa this has long been a distinguishing feature of the struggle for liberation. Many of the greatest leaders of the liberation struggle were committed Christians, including Albert Luthuli, Robert Sobukwe and Oliver and Adelaide Tambo. It is impossible to fully understand the history of the struggle for justice in South Africa without an understanding of the role of Christian leaders, individuals and organisations. Certainly the Christian church has much in its history which has actively supported and even directly caused the oppression of black people. But alongside this there is the story of leaders like Trevor Huddleston, Beyers Naudé, Desmond Tutu and many, many others, who stood, often at great cost, for truth and for justice.

The importance of holding a depth of Christian spirituality together with radical activism and obedience was recognised by Desmond Tutu when he became archbishop of Cape Town in 1986. Together with Revd Francis Cull, the archbishop set up the Institute for Christian Spirituality, which was based at Bishopscourt, the archbishop's home in Cape Town. Denise Ackermann was a member of the core team at the Institute, and she describes Desmond Tutu's rationale for establishing it in these words, 'If we can only get the clergy back at prayer, we will win the day.'[4]

Ackermann goes on to say that she did not for a moment believe that the archbishop was saying that the clergy had given up on prayer:

What he had in mind was an enduring truth for the life of the church. During the turbulent time of the 80s (and for that matter at all times), the church was/is called to stand for an alternative way of being a human community. As wave upon wave of repression, fuelled by states of emergency, were the order of the day in the 80s, as people's human dignity was trampled on by the forces of the state, the church, as the body of Christ, has a prophetic witness to proclaim tolerance, love, justice and the affirmation of the inviolable worth and dignity of all people. This required people of faith to draw deeply on their spiritual and moral resources. The Arch, with unfaltering wisdom, knew that the church, in order to live up to its prophetic task, needed members who could live creatively between the tension of vital public actions of protest against injustice on the one hand, and times of quiet withdrawal for prayer, on the other.[5]

Archbishop Tutu understood the importance, particularly for clergy and Christian leaders, of both contemplation and the struggle for justice. These are both imperatives of the gospel. The church in every generation needs leaders and people who are able to creatively hold these two together in their own lives. This is what then becomes the contemplative struggle.

Tutu and Cull also recognised the dangers of pursuing one of these and neglecting the other, as Ackermann says:

Both knew that burnout was too easily the lot of political and social activism. Both understood that withdrawal into a privatised world of self-involved spirituality was contrary to the teachings of Jesus Christ. Both knew that activism can be engaged more easily than taking time off to be with God. I believe that what the Arch and Francis had in mind was to assist the church – its clergy and its laity – to find the balance between active participation in the cause of justice and the life of prayer. In other words, we were to engage in the business of nurturing Christian spirituality in the life of the church.[6]

This book is an account of my own experience in responding to the call to radical discipleship. It is also an exploration of how this way of life may be rooted and sustained through an ever-deepening relationship of love with God. The question that many of us are wrestling with is this: what does it mean to be held firm in Christ in the centre of our being and to live with integrity in the 21st century?

In the life of Jesus himself, we see both regular withdrawal into solitude and prayer – the contemplative dimension – and radical action to heal and save people who were suffering and oppressed. This led him directly into conflict and struggle, and to his arrest, trial and death on a cross.

In the first part of this book, I reflect on my experience of growing up in South Africa in the 1950s and 1960s, and then as a student activist in the 1970s. In the second part, I look at the contemplative core of the life of Christian discipleship and also the challenges for radical obedience in our own age. I look in particular at the issues of climate change, racism, poverty and inequality, and war. I also reflect on the pressure that many people are dealing with each day because of digital technology and the age of acceleration. It seems to me that there is much that we can learn in facing the challenges of our own time from the experience of those who have already been through the fire of struggle and testing. The South African struggle for justice and liberation, in particular, has much to teach us as we make our way through the enormous global challenges of life in the 21st century.

Part One

The pearl of great price: seeking the kingdom of God

Again, the kingdom of heaven is like a merchant in search of fine pearls; on finding one pearl of great value, he went and sold all that he had and bought it.

MATTHEW 13:45–46

1

The contemplative struggle

In January 1958, when I was six years old, I was taken to the hostel at Central School, Potchefstroom, in what was then the eastern Transvaal of South Africa. My mum and dad unpacked my suitcase, said goodbye and drove away, leaving me with a small group of other boys who had little or no comprehension of what had just happened to us. That was the day I started boarding school. The next eleven years of my life were to be stamped indelibly with the constraints and control of the patterns of boarding school life. My whole adult life has to some extent been shaped by what happened on that summer day in Potchefstroom so many years ago.

Many children who have been sent to boarding school will tell similar stories. Some have been deeply traumatised by their experiences; others will speak positively of character formation and new opportunities. For myself, I found ways to survive, but I certainly did not thrive. Those were tough days. The first two or three days at Central School I was uncontrollably homesick and cried for hours and hours. The head teacher, Mr Martindale, and his wife were very kind and took me into their home for a short while until I had adjusted sufficiently to be able to move to the hostel. Gradually I adjusted to a life of bells, routines and boarding school food (mutton stew, cabbage and pumpkin, jelly and custard, melon and ginger jam). We caught crabs in the canal using long pieces of grass. I started writing letters home every week, a habit which was to last for many, many years. Every week there would be a letter from my mum: 'Hello darling...' I knew that my mother and father loved me very much; I just wasn't going to see much of them for the next eleven years.

L.P. Hartley famously wrote, 'The past is a foreign country; they do things differently there.'[7] The 1950s was the world of Elvis Presley, Connie Francis, Ricky Nelson and Doris Day. It was the world of ice-cream sodas, comics and bioscope (cinema), of long car journeys on dusty roads for two small boys, me and my brother, in the back of my father's Hillman Minx. In those days I lived in a boy's world, where my imagination was rich and alive but my understanding was limited. As an adult I find that the tables have been turned: these days I think too much and daydream too little. But in recent years I have found myself wanting to go back, on a journey to the past. Who was that little boy sitting on the steps of the school hostel in Potchefstroom? Why did his life turn out the way it has?

Although I had no idea of this at the time, I was growing up in a world where tectonic forces of change were building up. These would inevitably bring conflict and challenge to all those around me. In South Africa in the 1950s and 1960s, the policy of apartheid was being enforced with increasing brutality. The National Party had come to power in 1948 with an ideology of separate development for all the race groups living in South Africa. In 1960 the Sharpeville massacre took place – 69 people were killed and 180 injured as the police opened fire on a crowd of people who were protesting the pass (reference book) laws. I have no remembrance of this; I was only nine at the time. But I do remember the headlines in the Sunday papers about John Harris and the bomb blast at the Johannesburg railway station in 1964 which killed one person. Harris was found guilty of murder and hanged on 1 April 1965. The Rivonia trial, which led to the imprisonment of Nelson Mandela and other African National Congress (ANC) leaders, also took place around that time. I didn't understand what was going on; this was simply part of the background to my childhood and years of adolescence.

When I finally left boarding school in December 1968, everything changed. I had been nurtured in a simple Christian faith by my mother, who had taught me to say my prayers every night before I went to sleep and who read me Bible stories when I was little. My parents were occasional churchgoers, and at boarding school in Potchefstroom I went along to Sunday school at the local Anglican church. Being sent to boarding school was for me like being thrown into the deep end of a swimming pool. I had to hold on to whatever I could find that would give me a sense of safety and security, of being loved and cared for. I knew my need of God, and I did not doubt his reality or his love for me. I said my prayers, religiously, every night before I went to sleep.

Within a few weeks of leaving school, I was in the South African army, doing my national service, which was mandatory for all young white South African men at that time. I was fortunate in that I was able to do this in the same year that I started my university degree, as part of a unit called the Commandos. This sounds impressive, but the Commandos in South Africa at that time were not a group of hardened fighters but a bunch of fresh-faced 17- and 18-year-olds who were just doing what by law they were required to do before they could get on with the rest of their lives.

It was when I arrived at the University of Natal in Pietermaritzburg in 1969 that my life changed radically. Within six years I experienced first-hand some of the cost of opposing the powerful forces of the apartheid government. I saw my friends arrested, placed under five-year banning orders, detained without trial and scattered. The organisation in which I was a member of the local committee, the UCM, was crushed by the government during these years.

For a time I lost my way; I was scared, floundering and bewildered. Somehow, by the grace of God, I came to a new sense of the truth of the gospel of the kingdom of God in Jesus Christ. By 1974 I had been accepted by the local bishop as an Anglican ordinand and was preparing to begin my theological training for the ordained Anglican ministry. I had arrived at university in 1969 to study law and business administration. At that point in my life the idea of becoming an ordained priest in the Anglican Church had never crossed my mind. But everything changed during those years from 1969 to 1975. A verse that became a guiding principle of my life was 'Seek first the kingdom of God and His righteousness, and all these things shall be added to you' (Matthew 6:33, NKJV).

I had come to believe that my first call was to serve God, to know him and to love him, and to give my life as a faithful disciple of Jesus. Inextricably part of this was the call to commit myself to the struggle for justice in my own land. And so I determined that I would work in whatever way I could to resist and to bring an end to the appalling policy of apartheid. This I see now as a call which brings together the two central themes of the gospels, in particular the gospel of John. There is the 'inward' call to know God, to love him and give ourselves wholly to him. Alongside this there is the 'outward' call to serve our neighbour, whoever that may be. We find this in each of the four gospels. The first and greatest commandment is to love the Lord our God with all our hearts and souls and minds; the second commandment, which Jesus says is like it, is to love our neighbours as ourselves (see Matthew 22:37–40). To be a follower of Jesus means to seek to obey both of these commandments, and Jesus says, 'On these two commandments hang all the law and the prophets' (v. 40).

The contemplative heart

The gospel of John contains at its core these two great themes. We are to abide in Jesus, who loves us just as the Father has loved him and who abides in us (John 15:9). This is the call to know God, to dwell and rest in his love and to find in him our true security, our peace and our hope for the future. This points to the contemplative dimension of the gospel.

A contemplative heart is one which is rooted and held firm in the love of God and which increasingly sees the world as God sees it. This is all about knowing that 'God is love, and those who abide in love abide in God, and God abides in them' (1 John 4:16). To be contemplative is to be someone whose daily practice is a wordless resting in God beyond all our thoughts and words and strivings. It is abiding in the love of God no matter what life brings.

Alongside this is the theme of struggle, of conflict and costly obedience, of light and darkness. In the prologue to the gospel of John (1:1–18), we are told that although the light and life of God had come into the world in the person of Jesus, the world did not know him and his own did not receive him: 'The light shines in the darkness and the darkness did not comprehend it' (v. 5, NKJV).

If we are to abide in the love of Jesus for us, we are told that we must obey his commands. Above all, Jesus says, 'This is my commandment, that you love one another as I have loved you' (John 15:12). The example of love that Jesus has set us is a love that has no boundaries, no limits. It is an unconditional, freely given, unfailing love for all people and for all of creation. It is the love that is willing to die for those we serve and care for: 'No one has greater love than this, to lay down one's life for one's friends' (John 15:13).

My experience in South Africa in the 1970s brought together these two great themes of the gospel: contemplation and struggle. It is impossible for me to envisage a form of obedience to Christ that does not involve both of these dimensions. In the past we have seen churches and groups of Christians who have chosen one dimension and neglected or ignored the other.

A pietistic or salvation-centred approach may focus almost exclusively on bringing people to be saved by Jesus, but with no mention of the need to confront injustice and evil in the structures of our society. Among white South Africans in the 1970s and 1980s there was considerable appetite for this kind of Christianity. Many white South Africans wanted a faith that would provide comfort and reassurance, but they did not want to hear challenging and uncomfortable messages about the evils of apartheid and the need for Christians to act in response to what was happening in our society. Those of us who were seeking to be obedient to Jesus in confronting the darkness in our land often faced opposition and biting criticism from other white Christians and churches.

For those who are caught up in the demands and the powerful emotions of the struggle, there is always the danger of neglecting or losing the contemplative dimension. It may be hard to keep on praying and trusting in God when our friends are in jail, when people are dying and homes are burning, and when the oppressors seem to get away scot-free. We may rail at God; some may give up on God altogether. A number of psalms describe how this feels:

> Do not be silent, O God of my praise.
> For wicked and deceitful mouths are opened against me,
>   speaking against me with lying tongues.
> They beset me with words of hate,
>   and attack me without cause.
> In return for my love they accuse me,
>   even while I make prayer for them.
> PSALM 109:1–4

We cry out to God, but nothing seems to change. The lies and the oppression continue unchecked around us. Sometimes, perhaps often, it seems that God is silent while the wicked prosper and the innocent suffer. This is certainly how many of us felt in South Africa in the 1970s and 1980s. It was hard to keep going, to keep hoping and trusting in God that righteousness and justice would prevail and that the oppressors would be removed from their positions of power. The church in South Africa in those days was blessed with outstanding leaders who did not give up, but who continued through all the trials and testing to point to the hope that is ours in Christ Jesus. Archbishop Desmond Tutu is perhaps the most well known of these leaders, but he was not the only one. Again and again, Archbishop Tutu would stand up at large gatherings and at the funerals of those who had been murdered in the violence and proclaim the hope that we have in Christ Jesus. He would declare that goodness is stronger than evil, that love is stronger than hate, that light is stronger than darkness, and that life is and always will be stronger than death. 'Victory is ours through him who loves us,' he said, again and again, in the teeth of great darkness and heartbreaking tragedy.

'If I have to go to jail'

On one occasion when Desmond Tutu was bishop of Johannesburg, he joined Father James Mabaso and other clergy in conducting the funeral of a 16-year-old girl, Elizabeth Khumalo, in Daveyton township, outside Johannesburg. Elizabeth was one of four young people killed in a clash with police and troops after another funeral two weeks earlier. A news report from the *Los Angeles Times* describes what happened:

> Hundreds of police officers and soldiers, their weapons held ready, arrived during the funeral service... [They] surrounded the 1,000 mourners and ordered them to disperse rather than make the customary march to the cemetery for burial.
>
> In English and Afrikaans, the police announced that the gathering was illegal and warned that they were preparing to 'take action against those who refuse' to leave.
>
> Tutu then negotiated with the authorities to allow the funeral to proceed. Under a compromise worked out by Tutu and Lt. Col. G.H. Nel, the divisional police commander, the Daveyton town council supplied seven buses to take mourners the short distance to the cemetery for the burial so that they complied with the new funeral regulations imposed under South Africa's state of emergency...
>
> As Tutu, a solitary figure in his purple cassock, negotiated in a dusty field for half an hour with Nel, who was flanked by soldiers and backed by armoured cars, the mourners began freedom chants and jeered at the police and combat troops who surrounded them. Military helicopters circled overhead, and several times, a clash seemed almost inevitable...

Curiously Tutu had just defied the ban on political state-
ments by denouncing the restrictions on funerals, the 17-day-
old state of emergency and South Africa's whole system of racial
separation with his usual vehemence. During his remarks at the
funeral service, he challenged the government to arrest him.

'I do not want to go to jail,' he told the mourners, 'but if I have
to go to jail for preaching the gospel of our Lord, Jesus Christ,
so be it.'[8]

These were terrible times. A great storm was gathering in our land, and
nobody knew when it would end or what the outcome would be. As we
now know, all of this was leading up to those momentous days of April
1994, when South Africa held its first democratic elections and Nelson
Mandela became the nation's first black president. The decades leading up to this extraordinary transformation were times of trial and
pain, times of refining and testing, when I saw many examples of great
courage and self-sacrifice for the sake of others. I was a parish priest
in KwaZulu-Natal during this time and will never forget some of the
experiences we went through. I often think of people that I knew and
shared my life with. Their examples continue to inspire me and have,
I believe, much to teach us in the challenges that we now face as we
head deep into the world of the 21st century.

Archbishop Tutu is one of these. He is a contemplative, a man deeply
rooted in daily prayer and contemplative practice, whose heart is held
firm in the love of God which is ours in Christ Jesus. He is also a man
who has committed his life to speak and act for those who are victims
of injustice, exploitation and poverty. In the lives of people such as
Desmond Tutu, we can see something of what it may mean for us to be
true followers of Jesus Christ in our own time. This will surely involve
both contemplation and struggle.

My own faith and vocation were forged in the crucible of apartheid
South Africa. Some of us who were white South African Christians
chose to serve Christ in a way which led us into direct confrontation

with the powers of the state. We faced enormous pressure to conform to what was considered acceptable and safe by white South African society. Some died, some were imprisoned, some were given five-year banning orders, some became conscientious objectors in refusing to take up arms. For many of us, the requirement of obedience to Jesus Christ in our society meant that such possibilities had to be faced.

The question Jesus asks each one of us is the question he asked Simon Peter at the end of the gospel of John: 'Simon son of John, do you love me more than these?' (John 21:15). All of us who call ourselves Christians face powerful and seductive challenges to our discipleship and obedience. If we choose to say, like Peter, 'Yes, Lord; you know that I love you', then we will need to look hard at what this means for us in our society and in the strange and broken world of the 21st century.

2

Growing up

I like to think that I grew up on a farm. Of course, most of my life in those growing-up years was spent at boarding school, around 200 miles away from Brownlow, the farm where we lived, but I have many good memories of it. This was the world that I called home. Somehow, to this day, my deepest sense of home is a place like the farm where I grew up: peaceful and safe, knowing I was loved and cared for, at one with nature and the beauty of creation.

The truth is that life on the farm was far from ideal. It was a hard life for my parents. The farm was always heavily in debt, and trips to the bank manager were a regular occurrence. We suffered crippling droughts, weeks and weeks of looking up at the sky and longing desperately for rain. There were terrible fires that swept across from neighbouring farms, driven by the strong Berg winds which blew for days on end. Often in my school holidays we would be out burning firebreaks, beating down the smouldering grass and putting out the flames wherever they flared up. The heat and the smoke would sting my eyes and face and saturate my hair. But I was out with the men, doing hard, physical work, and I felt alive growing up on a farm.

As we grow older, we learn more of the truth about ourselves and about the world around us. We may also, if we are open to this, find ourselves learning more about God and the truth of his immeasurable love written into every facet and corner of his creation. My childhood understanding of the world and of God was full of wonder and rich in imagination, but I could only see what was before me. I had little idea of the wider context of things, of what was really going on in my parents' lives, in the country or in the wider world.

We were living in a world of rapid change, of social and political upheaval and of extraordinary technological achievements. In 1969, on the day that Neil Armstrong and Buzz Aldrin first walked on the moon, my father told the Zulu men who worked on the farm with him that two American men had walked on the moon earlier that day. They were incredulous. They knew about aeroplanes, machines of the white man that fly through the air – *ibanoyi* – but flying to the moon? How could this be?

In the days of my childhood there was no television. We sometimes switched on the radio in the evenings to listen to the news and the game show *Pick-a-Box*. But apart from this, we made our own entertainment. Our world was not greatly impinged upon by what was happening in America or Europe. It seems to me now, when our lives are bombarded each day by infotainment and advertising, that I would love to go back to the lost and seemingly innocent world of my youth. On that day in 1969 when two men walked on the moon, the Zulu workers on our farm were astounded to hear news of an event from far, far away that said that all of our lives were going to change, whether we liked it or not. Technology is taking over the world. But we did not know what this was to mean, for our lives or for our planet.

Technology in itself is neither good nor bad; how we use the technology is what matters. But the digital and globalised world in which we now live presents complex challenges not only to those who seek to follow the teachings of Jesus; all of humanity is now faced with a world which has been created around us, where very powerful forces are at work. Many of us are now exposed to these influences from early childhood, and it is almost impossible to escape from them. It may be helpful and important to see that in this new world of the 21st century, there is much wisdom and truth from the past that remains valid and necessary. For me, revisiting the world of my childhood is one way I can gain understanding of how I might live as a human being made in the image of God in the extraordinary world of the 21st century.

Life on the farm

As I go back in my mind to those days on the farm, I feel that I am reaching out to a part of myself that I have largely lost, and which I need to find again. For us children on the farm – my brother, my little sister and me – time was empty during our school holidays. One day flowed into the next. We got up when it was light and in the evenings we had our supper together, read our books or comics and went to bed. The nights were long and could be inky black. There was no extraneous light from anywhere, only the moon and the stars. There was no sound of machines or engines, only the silence of a sleeping world. The days were spent roaming around. We were free to go wherever we liked. The nearest town was about ten miles away, on the other side of the mountain pass. So buying things or going shopping was never something we thought about when we were growing up. We had time, and we had freedom. Adult life was something far off, beyond the horizon. All we knew was what we had.

I would go for long walks, down to the Buffalo River or up to Laing's Nek battlefield at the top of the farm. Our farm (my father was the manager not the owner) was in northern Natal on the slopes of Majuba mountain. The top of Majuba was where the British forces were defeated by the Boers, in the key battle of the first Boer War (1880–81). This was preceded by the battle of Laing's Nek, and when I was a boy there were still bullets and shell casings and other bits and pieces from the battle lying in the grass, waiting to be picked up by small boys or souvenir hunters. The Buffalo River, which formed the eastern boundary of the farm, is a large river inaccessible by road for miles around. It ran through deep rocky cliffs where we would go to pick bags of prickly pears to take home and eat. There were two streams running through a forest, down to the Buffalo River, with two large waterfalls. In the summer I could go down to the waterfall and play in the water while the dassies (rock rabbits) watched from the rocks above. In the winter some of the pools of water froze solid, and we would go down and try to break the ice with sticks and stones.

There was not much money, so to a large extent we lived off the land. We had milk and cream from the cows, and we made our own butter. We grew our own vegetables and fruit. Most of our meat came from the farm, with eggs from the chickens. If my mother wanted roast chicken for Sunday lunch, she would say to the Zulu women who worked in our kitchen, 'Trifina, Gertrude, *bulala nkuku* [kill a chicken].' Gertrude would catch a chicken and hold its head down over a wooden block near the kitchen door, and Trifina would chop off its head with an axe. The headless chicken would run around in ever-decreasing circles until it died. My mother preferred not to be around when this was going on, so normally this would happen on a Friday morning when my parents made their weekly trip to town. But my brother and sister and I would stand and watch, until the chicken was dead and taken away for plucking. This was farm life. There was not much to be squeamish about.

When we arrived at the farm there was no electricity and we depended on paraffin lamps at night, with batteries for the radio and torches. But soon Dad bought a lighting plant and a bank of batteries, and every evening just before dark he would start up the lighting plant and charge the batteries. For water, we depended on springs further up the hill which fed a reservoir in the farmyard. When the water level in the reservoir started to fall during the droughts, we became preoccupied with conserving water. The three of us children all shared the same bath, and only a hand's depth of water was allowed.

We were not the only family living on our farm. There were around six Zulu families who lived at the top of the farm, near the Laing's Nek battlefield. They had their own cattle and land for crops. My recollection is that my father always treated the men who worked for us with respect and dignity. My mother was a nurse, and she would provide medicines and medical help when it was needed. At the end of every month the men were paid their wages, which I'm sure was not much even compared to the little that Dad was getting as farm manager.

Although my family's relationship with the Zulu families was, as I recall, friendly, trusting and courteous, this was not the norm in our area. I remember being shocked at seeing a neighbouring farmer beating a Zulu man with a big stick outside his farm shed. I was there as a guest, to play with his son, who was a friend of mine. I knew immediately that what I was seeing was wrong, partly because this would never have happened on our farm. But as I look back, I can see that the whole situation in which I grew up was shot through with problematic and painful assumptions. What were we doing on that land in the first place? Why was it 'our farm', and not the farm of the Zulu people who lived there long before we or any other white families had even been there? This was not really our land at all. And, even by the standards of those days, we had so much and they had so little. We were the masters, and they were the servants. Looking back, it all feels very uncomfortable.

This was the world that I knew as home. As a child I accepted it and took it for granted, not knowing that it would all disappear so quickly. By the time I was in my early 20s, my parents could no longer cope with the relentless financial problems, the threats of fire and drought, the isolation and the endless difficulties of farm life. The children were no longer at home, so my parents left and the farm was sold. A few years after we left the farm, my father said to me, out of the blue one day, that the thing which troubled him most about leaving the farm was thinking about what might have happened to our farm workers and their families after we had gone. Their way of life on the farm would surely come to an end, and they would be scattered to who knows where.

A time of being my true self

I will always be grateful for those days growing up on Brownlow, my home for 14 years. Now, many years later, I find myself being drawn to explore and to rediscover the contemplative dimension to life where being is more important than getting things done and achieving goals. I know that this is something that was once as natural to me as breathing. I have known days and weeks when all my life was playing and being and finding out. I was one with the natural world. It was part of my identity, and I revelled in it. I took on its dangers and risks, and my parents gave me the freedom to work out the limits of what I could and could not do. If I became ill or hurt myself, that was all part of life's learning.

To be contemplative is to return in our inmost being to the person that God has made us to be. It is to let go of all the egocentric, self-conscious demands of adult life and to become, again, our true selves. Was I ever more my true self than when I was playing down at the stream on the farm or lying in the forest under the trees with arms spread wide, just gazing up at the beauty of the leaves and the dancing light of the deep, dark forest world? I was free, one with the universe, with all of God's creation, hearing and responding to its voices in a way that is almost impossible for me now.

I have said that the farm was home, the place where I knew that I belonged, that I was loved and cared for. But most of my life was spent away from the farm, at boarding school. I would long for school holidays, when I could 'go home'. During the school term, I counted the weeks and the days until the holidays began. I hated going back to boarding school when the holidays came to an end.

I now recognise that, although I felt loved and cared for at home, my parents were going through their own struggles. No parent is able to love their child with a completely unconditional and unblemished love. My father had spent most of his 20s fighting in the desert of north Africa in World War II. He was in the armoured car division of the Sixth Army. We still have his 'desert rat' emblem, which was sewn into his army uniform. I am sure that he had been traumatised during the war; he was prone to outbursts of anger and, I suspect, prolonged but undiagnosed depression. This made for some difficult times for all of us.

As a boy I loved to spend time riding with my dad in the truck or sitting with him in his workshop on the farm, but he was often moody and uncommunicative. He wanted to be a good father, but there was something in him that made building a close father–son relationship very difficult for him. He tried hard, and we had some good times together, but there were also many times when he simply could not reach out beyond himself to respond with understanding to this young boy with an enquiring mind who was his son.

When I was ten, in May 1961, I ran away from school. I had been moved to boarding school in Pietermaritzburg, then the capital of the province of Natal. It was a Sunday afternoon, and I and a friend called Brian had gone out for the afternoon, which we were allowed to do. We had changed into home clothes at another friend's house, and for some reason I got the idea that it would be an adventure to run away from school and go to Durban, where maybe we could get on board a ship in the harbour. This was not in any way premeditated; it was just a spur-of-the-moment idea of a ten-year-old boy who hated boarding school and had been reading lots of boys' adventure stories. So we walked down to the main road to Durban, Brian and I, and we put out our thumbs to hitch a ride. After a while we were picked up by a man in an American Rambler car. He asked us some questions about what we were doing and where we were headed. About ten miles from Pietermaritzburg, he stopped at a roadhouse called the Log Cabin at Cato Ridge and phoned the police. That was the end of our great adventure.

We were taken back to school, and the next day we were both in the head teacher's office. Our punishment was four cuts with the cane, and a gating for the rest of term. He also wrote to our parents to tell them what had happened.

A few days later I received a letter from my father. He wrote:

> My dear Ian,
> I had a letter yesterday from Mr Evans telling me that you tried to run away from school on Sunday. He said that you claimed that you were homesick and wanted to see your parents. Seeing that he is punishing you, I am not going to do anything more

about that side of it, but as I don't think you realised what your action might lead to, I am going to explain some of its results.

My father seldom wrote to me at school, but this was a long letter in which he said that I was lying about being homesick and that he and my mother were terribly upset about what I had done. 'It would break our hearts to think that you were growing up to be a duck-tail or a teddy-boy or a tramp or anything of that sort,' he wrote.

I was stunned. I wept and put the letter away, and I have kept it to this day. From that moment I knew that I had no option at all but to fit in, do what I was told and make the best of it. From then until I completed my schooling, I simply had to survive, conform and respect those in authority. That also was the world in which I grew up.

Revisiting times and events like this is costly and painful, yet to find again the true self and the peace that passes understanding, we have to be willing to return to the sources of our pain and let that pain pass through our adult hearts. I know now that God's love for me is complete and unconditional. I have no sense at all of anger or bitterness towards Dad. I know that he loved me, but he had his own troubles and pain to deal with, and his response to me was often tainted by this. So I find that as I bring all my childhood, my growing-up years, before the God of love, I increasingly know his healing, his smile as he looks upon me and a new contentment with being the person he made me. I know that God looks on me, and on all these events that formed me, with unfailing compassion and mercy. Our God is not the God of condemnation, guilt and shame. He is the God who sets us free to become all that he intends us to be, to be fully alive in Christ.

To be contemplative means to daily bring our hearts and all that is within them into the presence of God. Here we find that Jesus says to us again and again, 'Peace I leave with you; my peace I give to you. I do not give to you as the world gives. Do not let your hearts be troubled, and do not let them be afraid' (John 14:27). It's okay. All is well, and all will be well.

As we continue in this practice, we become aware in new ways of the sources of our inner restlessness, anxiety, losses and regrets. As these surface, we will be able to look again at some of the times and events in our lives that have left unresolved scars and pain in our hearts. We find that we can do this because we know the peace of God which passes understanding. We find that his peace and his unfailing compassion are able to come in new ways into our hearts, into our deepest being, and make us new.

3

The University Christian Movement

One of the things that first attracted me to the University Christian Movement (UCM) was the worship. It was completely different to anything I had experienced up to that point in my life. I was familiar with the Anglican prayer book, with hymns and school prayers. Most of this I found seriously boring, as did almost all of my peers. But UCM worship was informal and fresh and full of interesting and exciting ideas. Above all, there was freedom. This was 1969 and this, I knew, was the future, and I wanted to be part of it.

I had arrived at the University of Natal in Pietermaritzburg in February 1969 to study commerce and law. During freshers' week I joined UCM and started to attend their weekly meetings. We met in the chaplain's room on the campus, sitting on beanbags and cushions, which was a whole new idea back then. We listened to music – Bob Dylan and Joan Baez – we sang, we danced, we prayed, we shared agape meals of bread and wine. There were slide shows on the wall and posters and guitars and tambourines. God was speaking to my generation! We sang 'Shosholoza', the song that became famous years later during the Rugby World Cup in South Africa in 1995, and we danced around the room together with our hands on each other's shoulders, singing:

Shosholoza, Shosholoza
Ku lezontaba
Stimela Siphume e South Africa
Wena uyabaleka
Wena uyabaleka lezontaba
Stimela Siphume e South Africa

We were told that the song was sung by migrant workers travelling on the packed steam trains across South Africa to work in the mines and factories. It is an African song of struggle, hardship and togetherness.

UCM was in existence in South Africa for just five years, from 1967 to 1972. When I joined at the beginning of 1969, UCM was thriving, but the government soon became alarmed at some of its activities, and the organisation was ruthlessly crushed. Many of the leaders were detained, banned or fled the country. This was the crucible in which my own understanding of the Christian faith was formed. This was not formal, institution-based Christianity. This was something fresh, dynamic and challenging. This was about seeking God, the real God; not just the God of the white South African church, but the God who made us all and who loves us all, regardless of race, gender, nationality or anything else. This was also about struggle. Even when I joined UCM in 1969, there was an awareness among the leadership that members of the organisation were being closely watched and all its activities were being tabulated. It was only a matter of time before the storm would break and the members would be scattered.

The UCM of South Africa came into being in 1967. It was formed by a group of mainline churches, including the Anglican, Methodist, Presbyterian, Congregational and Roman Catholic churches. The intention was to establish 'an ecumenical, non-racial Christian mission in the academic world across South Africa'.[9] For the first two or three years there was extraordinary growth and vitality in this new organisation. An experimental worship service on one campus in May 1968 attracted 450 students out of a student body of 1,500. UCM was undoubtedly making a real impact among students and young people.

Some people in South Africa would have said that I and my friends were being radicalised by UCM. In a sense this was true, because when I joined, UCM offered us a community which was intent on working out together the real meaning of Christian discipleship. At freshers' week, I was given a leaflet at the UCM stand that was entitled 'Over to you'. It set out, in English and Afrikaans, what the UCM of Southern African was all about:

'What return can I make to the Father for all his goodness to me?'
What am I now doing on the campus, in the town, through the country and over the world?
Do I spread his gospel of truth to those in ignorance, apathy and error?
Do I extend his love in the face of prejudice, loneliness, injustice and oppression?
Do I rejoice in Christian hope before cynics, the embittered and disillusioned?
Do I strive to repair the divisions and conflicts between churches, between peoples, between parties and blocs?

'Cut off from me you can do nothing.'
On your own you are helpless and just useless, but...
MEET with other Christians of all denominations
WORSHIP jointly on your campus
STUDY together, accepting Christ's message no matter by whom it is spoken
CO-OPERATE with both staff and students in common witness to Christ
WORK with fellow students both intelligently and with all your strength
SERVE both within the university and especially the under-privileged outside
OPEN yourself to new initiatives, following together the Holy Spirit
DEVELOP the world's human and natural resources – yourself included – for peace
THANK God for all that he has provided you with
then you know...

'Where two or three are gathered together in my name, there I am in the midst of them.'[10]

It is astonishing to me to read this now and to realise how radical this turned out to be in the context of South Africa in the late 1960s and early 1970s. The call to respond to the goodness of God the Father and to spread the gospel of truth in Christ is not something to be taken lightly. The only way that this message will be acceptable to those who are opposed to truth and justice will be if the message is so watered down that it presents no threat to them whatsoever.

Dangerous radicals

To be radical is to cut through the superficial and the illusory to find the truth and to act upon it. Jesus is the true radical, because he is the way, the truth and the life (John 14:6). 'Sanctify them in the truth; your word is truth,' said Jesus (John 17:17). The question facing those who call themselves Christian in our own age is: what does it mean to be true and radical disciples of Jesus in the 21st century?

I believe there is much that we can learn in our present situation from the experience of UCM in South Africa. UCM set out to offer young people the possibility of becoming a community of radical disciples of Jesus in a world that in many ways had set its face against the values of the kingdom of God. We were idealistic and full of hope, excitement and joy. We sensed that, although we were a small group, we were part of the future. We saw a vision of a non-racial South Africa, where we would all work together to build a nation that would shine as a beacon around the world. We were talking about things that really mattered, and we were committed to action, to doing something to bring change. We believed in a different future for our country from everything that was being presented to us as the norm, as 'the way it is'.

But soon we were facing serious opposition. We were being portrayed in the media as communist-inspired troublemakers, as dangerous radicals. We were infiltrated at every level by informers and by security police members. I now believe that by 1970 at least half of our local UCM committee were Security Branch informers. Our leaders were banned, detained and scattered. The whole organisation was under severe pressure. Many cracks appeared, and by 1972 UCM was finished. We should not underestimate the strength of the forces that are opposed to truth and justice and the reign of Christ and his kingdom. If we are serious about obedience to Jesus, we will face opposition and persecution, as surely as Jesus himself did. This is the cost of true discipleship.

My experience at UCM etched these lessons into my heart at a young and impressionable age. I did not have the chance to think of being a follower of Jesus as a safe and comfortable option. I quickly came to see that those who use Christianity as a means of gaining blind comfort and false security are a massive obstacle to the good news of Jesus and the witness of the church. To follow Jesus is to oppose all the forces of injustice and evil that cause human suffering, poverty and pain. If we look at the gospel record of the life of Jesus himself, we see that his whole ministry was marked by this kind of confrontation and conflict.

I remember a tutor at my theological college some years later saying to me, 'Ian, never believe anything anyone tells you about the Christian faith unless it can be certainly found to be true in the life and teaching of Jesus.' At the beginning of his public ministry, Jesus declared his manifesto of the work which he had come to do:

> The Spirit of the Lord is upon me, because he has anointed me to bring good news to the poor. He has sent me to proclaim release to the captives and recovery of sight to the blind, to let the oppressed go free, and to proclaim the year of the Lord's favour.
> LUKE 4:18–19

In every chapter of the gospel of John there is challenge, confrontation and conflict. The gospel begins with the light of the world breaking into the darkness. We are told that Jesus came to his own people, 'and his own people did not accept him' (1:11). In chapter 2 Jesus drives the money changers and traders from the temple with a whip of cords (v. 15). The ministry of Jesus is an unfolding story of the clash of light and darkness (3:19–21), leading inexorably to the arrest and crucifixion of Christ, and thus to the victory of the resurrection. This narrative of conflict and suffering for righteousness' sake is absolutely central to the gospel.

Black consciousness

Our local branch of UCM held a regular weekly programme of Tuesday lunchtime meetings for Bible study and discussion in the chaplain's room, as well as bread-and-cheese lunches on Thursday to raise money for the local malnutrition relief fund, and Sunday evening worship 'happenings'. We were also involved in literacy training and in supporting work camps at a remote rural community health centre.

In July 1970 I attended the national UCM conference at Wilgespruit Fellowship Centre near Johannesburg. By this point, a new movement of black consciousness was emerging in the black universities. Steve Biko had been an active member of UCM, but he and other black leaders felt that it was now important for black students to form their own organisations where they would not be constantly dealing with a white political agenda. A South African Students' Organisation (SASO) document explained that 'it was felt that a time had come when Blacks had to formulate their own thinking, unpolluted by ideals emanating from a group with lots at stake in the status quo'.[11] SASO was formed in July 1969 as a black students' movement, following discussions at a previous UCM conference. This led to the founding of other black consciousness groups such as the Black Peoples' Convention, the Black Workers' Alliance and the Black Women's Movement. All of this was viewed by the government with mounting alarm.

Despite the emergence of black consciousness, there was no sense of a wholesale withdrawal of black students from UCM. Black leaders, such as Justice Moloto and Winkie Direko, continued to play significant roles in UCM. However, some white students started to think about the possibility of a white consciousness movement and what that might look like. Within UCM, black consciousness was seen by many students as an inevitable and appropriate response to the pressure placed on black people by white society. We were privileged to be among the few white South Africans who were able to hear first-hand accounts from black people of what life was like for them in apartheid South Africa.

The UCM conference in 1970 was called Encounter '70, and it had a significant impact on me. This was a large non-racial gathering of students from across South Africa with experimental worship, encounter groups, outdoor theatre and in-depth discussion. We looked at topics such as 'Is God white or black?' and other theological concerns, as well as having lengthy discussions about sexual freedom and morality and major sociopolitical issues. I was elected as publications officer for the Natal region.

I met some amazing people at this conference. Pat Horn was a student from the University of the Witwatersrand in Johannesburg. She was the same age as me and, like me, drawn to the ideals and vision that we saw in UCM and its leaders. After the conference I made a number of trips to Johannesburg to spend time with Pat. Some months later, I was shocked to read in the newspaper that Pat and some other UCM members had been arrested at a UCM seminar at an Anglican mission hospital in the northern Transvaal. The newspaper report said that they were arrested at 11.30 pm on Sunday and taken to the Groblersdal police station, where all of them, including the white girls, were stripped and searched, and then released at about 3.00 pm on the following Monday. The white students each had to pay 20-rand admission-of-guilt fines for being on Bantu Trust land without permission. The black students were fined 5 rand each for not having their reference (pass) books with them. This was pure intimidation. This was what we were increasingly up against.

I was now regularly taking part in silent protest vigils against the actions of the government. Small groups of students would stand at the main gates of the campus holding placards reading 'Return to the rule of law' and other similar slogans. Across the main road the security police (Special Branch) would park their cars in full view of the protestors, watching us and taking our photographs. Sometimes they would follow us as we walked to the shops, driving slowly behind us to send us an unmistakable message.

In May 1970 some 357 students were arrested in Johannesburg while taking part in a protest march. Thirty students were then formally charged and put on trial. While this was happening the students at my own university seemed completely apathetic. The National Union of South African Students (NUSAS) had called a national day of protest on 11 May 1970 to protest against the continued detention without trial of Winnie Mandela and 21 others. I was discussing all this with a friend in the men's residence. We decided we had to do something. We made a huge banner reading 'SILENCE IS ACCEPTANCE. PROTEST MAY 11?' I had keys to the Students' Union offices, so in the middle of the Sunday night we hung the banner across the front of the Students' Union building. As bleary-eyed students made their way to lectures on Monday morning they were confronted with the banner's message draped across the building.

Freedom '71

The UCM conference in July 1971 was called 'Freedom '71'. I was asked by Basil Moore, the general secretary of UCM, to be responsible for producing a daily news and information sheet during the conference to share ideas and stimulate discussion, as well as giving daily updates to the delegates on what was happening. I agreed to do this and headed home at the end of the June term for a few days' break before the conference started in early July.

There had been a number of articles in national newspapers about UCM and the Wilgespruit Centre. One Afrikaans newspaper had run a front-page story saying, 'The central point of the liberal onslaught against South Africa has been unmasked. It is the Wilgespruit Fellowship Centre on the West Rand.'[12] Other English-language newspapers had similar stories. Cabinet ministers were denouncing UCM and threatening to act against it.

When I arrived home, I told my parents that I would be going to the UCM conference in a few days' time. My father had been reading the news reports and told me that he did not want me to be involved with UCM in any way, including going to the conference. I said that I was already committed and had an important job to do. A huge argument ensued: I was determined to go, and my father was determined that I would not. It ended when my father told me that it was my decision, but if I decided to go to the UCM conference, I would not be welcome back home after that. I had to choose between UCM and my family.

I went to my bedroom, and I prayed desperately and thought about what to do. What could I do? It would break my mother's heart if I defied my father on this and caused a rift that might be very difficult to heal. The next morning I sent a telegram to Basil Moore saying that I was sorry but that I was not able to attend the conference. I was sad and I was embarrassed. I could not bring myself to tell anyone the real reason why I had bailed out. I just tried to put this behind me and press on. Only now am I able even to talk about what happened that night on the farm.

This was a battle that was very painful and this time my father had won. But he would not break my resolve to be the person that God was calling me to be and to do what I believed to be right before God. In fact, as events unfolded, my father was unfailingly supportive, and I do not for a moment doubt his deep love for me. Times such as these can stretch us to the very limit, and they can stretch our families and family relationships too. Sometimes we face hard choices, and it is so important in these moments of crisis that our hearts are ruled by love.

Working this out in practice is not easy. I understood then that we are called by God to love and to honour our fathers and our mothers. We have to trust, as we do this to the best of our ability, that God's will and purposes will be worked out in ways that we may not at the time be able to comprehend. To follow and obey Jesus will lead us to conflict and to struggle. But God is faithful, and we can trust in him to work in all things for good for those who love him and are called according to his purpose (see Romans 8:28). As Martin Luther King wrote:

Faith in the dawn arises from the faith that God is good and just. When one believes this, he knows that the contradictions of life are neither final nor ultimate. He can walk through the dark night with the radiant conviction that all things work together for good for those that love God. Even the most starless midnight may herald the dawn of some great fulfilment.[13]

4

Conflict and struggle

Freedom '71 took place without me in July 1971. It was, as things turned out, the final national conference of UCM. The emergence of black consciousness led to a discussion at Freedom '71 about the need for a white consciousness movement. This was concerned with the problem of being a white South African Christian living in the apartheid society. Some, the 'leavers', felt that the system was so restrictive that there was no meaningful alternative to leaving South Africa and building a new life somewhere else. Others, the 'stayers', saw the tensions involved in living in South Africa to be beneficial, forcing us to look hard at ourselves and our own attitudes, and to find ways within South African society to work for justice and to confront oppression.[14]

Another significant group that had emerged by this time was the women's liberation group. It was recognised that, for black women especially, female liberation and black liberation were inextricably linked. Neither struggle could succeed without the other. By the end of the 1971 conference, UCM had moved to the point of becoming a federation of projects, with the executive being simply a coordinating committee. The movement had by now changed fundamentally from the original UCM set up by the churches in 1967. Around this time all the constituent churches withdrew their support for UCM in one way or another. Many mainline church leaders and members had become alarmed by the reports they were reading and hearing about UCM's activities. There was concern about the new experimental forms of worship, about liberal theology and about the emphasis on encounter groups and the use of group dynamics to build relationships through small groups. This was all regarded as too radical for the institutional churches at that time. But the most serious problem was the growing confrontation with the apartheid government. The churches at that point were simply not ready to back a student organisation like UCM, which was unequivocally committed to challenging the political system and asking searching questions, particularly of those in positions of white power and privilege.

Soon after Freedom '71 a number of key UCM leaders were placed under five-year banning orders, which severely restricted their ability to travel, to publish or speak publicly and to meet with other people. In April 1972 a notice of dissolution was sent out, and UCM was dis-banded a few months later. The main reasons given for this decision were the withdrawal of support from the churches which 'has seriously affected our ability to speak in the university world from within and with the churches'[15] and pressure from the government, which was putting impossible strains on UCM. There was also an understanding that the existence of UCM as an organisation was 'probably standing in the way of the success of its own projects, particularly the Black Theology, the Literacy and the White Consciousness projects'.[16]

By 1972 UCM had been increasingly moving away from its Christian roots, especially in some of the thinking about sexual morality, mar-riage and family that was emerging at conference groups. There were also reports of immorality and un-Christian behaviour among mem-bers, although I myself did not see this, except for some drunkenness at one formation school. But UCM was an organisation under severe pressure, so it is not surprising that in these circumstances people did not always act in ways which were safe or sensible. It had become clear that the established churches had lost confidence in UCM and were no longer willing to defend us. Some members of UCM gave up on the church completely, and some lost their faith. Others of us found ourselves going through a time of wandering in the wilderness.

By 1971, as well as my involvement with UCM, I also became editor of *NUX*, the student newspaper for our university in Pietermaritzburg. This was a great opportunity for me. I loved the thrill of putting together the next edition and then seeing it come out, and watching the response as students picked up and read their hot-off-the-press new copies of *NUX*. We were students, and we were pushing the boundaries. South Africa in those days was a very conservative society. But this was 1971, and we were the Woodstock generation. We intended to be provocative, to question and to make people think.

I talked about this to a friend, and wondered whether it was better to be gentle, and try to persuade people to change their attitudes without upsetting them, or to confront them and provoke a reaction. My friend said, 'If you really shock a conservative, their first reaction will be one of complete rejection of the new ideas. But this will make them more receptive to these ideas. The next time they hear this they will be more prepared to hear what is being said. Your chances of moving the rabble are far greater by being radical than being mild.'

This is how many of us were thinking at that time. It is salutary for Christians to remember how unafraid Jesus was in confronting hypocrisy and hardness of heart. Jesus certainly did not back down because people might be offended or upset by the truth. It is not possible to uphold truth and justice without engaging in struggle and conflict.

'You might be okay, but...'

During my time as editor of *NUX*, we published a stream of articles and news items which raised important issues and drew attention to what was going on around us. From pollution and environmental action to detention without trial, from conscription and military service to malnutrition and poverty: this is what *NUX* was all about.

One article by a fellow commerce student, John Morrison, began with these words: 'You might be okay, but South Africa is in a bad way and time is running out if there is to be any hope of peaceful change.'[17] As I read John's article now, I am reminded of the message which young climate change activists are proclaiming in our own time: 'You might be okay, but our planet is in a bad way and time is running out.' There is a time to speak and a time to be silent. The danger for Christians is that, through fear or cowardice, we choose silence when we need to be speaking. In this situation we should remember silence is acceptance.

In August 1971 students from the Pietermaritzburg campus held demonstrations (called 'guerrilla theatre') that disrupted the Sunday services in two local churches. This caused a nationwide stir and widespread outrage. One of the leaders of the demonstrations was Jeremy Hurley, the local chairman of UCM and a good friend of mine. I asked Jeremy to write a front-page article for *NUX* explaining the thinking behind the demonstrations. He wrote:

> The world is in a state at the moment where the gap between rich and poor is widening all the time. In South Africa this is also true. New millionaires are made every day, as are thousands of poverty-stricken people. The church has an 80% black membership, which means in this country that almost 80% of the church is poor. How can the church hierarchy (consisting of the cardinal, archbishops, bishops and some priests) afford to buy huge mansions to live in, in often the most select suburbs?[18]

These words still have a powerful impact and resonance nearly 50 years later. The inequality gap between rich and poor continues to widen across much of our world. The Christian church has millions of members in Africa and South America who live in extreme poverty, and yet affluent Christians in the west often pursue lifestyles where expensive holidays, luxury cars and large, beautiful homes and gardens are seen as normal. If we take seriously the teaching of Jesus, there are some hard questions to be asked for many of us about all of this.

Jeremy Hurley was writing from direct experience of the views of young black South African students, many of whom had grown up in poverty. We had heard for ourselves at UCM the anger and the pain of black people. They had come to the realisation that white-led organisations, including churches, always saw the South African situation through the lens of their own self-interest and privilege. Their view of the white Christian church was that it was all too often part of the rich and powerful elite, more interested in maintaining the status quo than caring for the poor. They believed that the aspirations of black people were not being met by the white religious and theological establishment.

In the same year, 1971, Alpheus Zulu, the bishop of Zululand, wrote in a diocesan newsletter:

> Young concerned Christians are shocked by the drift from the church of young educated blacks, especially in the cities. They find the reason for this withdrawal a challenge to Christian leaders to demonstrate the relevance of Jesus Christ for black persons in apartheid and discriminating South Africa. They want black theologians to reply to the charge that Jesus is Lord and Saviour of the white people only.[19]

Jeremy also wrote:

> So who are the Christians? The churches who work within the law of the land (however un-Christian it may be) or the people who work within the law of love? The churches have to get back to living Christian lives, and they are obviously not allowed to do this by their very superstructure of authority. As far as I can see the only answer lies in forming small, religious communities outside the church structures and the books of rules. They could learn to live with and love each other. They could learn to love loving, and thereby God and humanity (for God IS Love).[20]

In South Africa at the time, this was radical stuff. Jeremy was saying that true Christianity is about obeying the law of love and that the institutional church had become a major obstacle to Christian action and obedience to Christ. This raises important questions for Christian faith and discipleship. We now live in a globalised world where rampant consumerism and digital technology control the minds and hearts of millions upon millions of people. What does obedience to the teaching of Jesus mean in the self-oriented, acquisitive way of life which so many of us are now buying into? Increasingly I see hope for the future not so much in what the institutional church is doing or saying but in small communities of Christians, often living in deprived areas, showing by their lives and their generosity and servanthood the hope that Jesus offers to the world.

In October 1971 I edited my last edition of *NUX*. The final exams for my degree were just a few weeks away. The edition was called the 'Reform Issue' and the front cover was a large photograph of students protesting with placards against police detentions, torture and deaths in police custody. We had previously handed out around 3,000 pamphlets in town to try to make the public more aware of police torture. This issue of *NUX* carried articles about authoritarianism and civil disobedience, women's liberation, the wages commission and the music of Frank Zappa. There was also a news item that Justice Moloto, the travelling secretary of UCM, had been banned. He was now restricted to Mafeking for five years. Earlier that year, in May, Justice Moloto had visited Natal and spent time with me on the campus. I still remember the looks of surprise and astonishment from other white students as I walked around openly talking with a black man as a friend and colleague. Many white students had never seen this before. Some clearly were not comfortable with this blatant challenge to our segregated world.

On the morning of 24 October 1971 I was woken at 4.00 am in my university residence room by a distressed lady warden and two security policemen in khaki overcoats. They had documents, including a search warrant, authorising them to search the premises of my room. The warrant stated that the magistrate had evidence of a reasonable suspicion that I was part of a conspiracy to overthrow the South African government by violence. This was completely untrue. I was dumbfounded. As I stood in my pyjamas, with the lady warden at the door, the security police went through the entire contents of my room. All my drawers were emptied, clothes were shaken out and dumped, all my books and notes were examined. I was not asked any questions and nothing incriminating was found. Later I discovered that this was part of a series of nationwide raids on students, church leaders and other anti-apartheid activists. Among those who were raided that morning were Philip Russell, bishop of Port Elizabeth, playwright Athol Fugard, Winnie Mandela and many of the leaders of UCM, NUSAS and SASO.

A few days later a special NUSAS newsletter was distributed across South African university campuses. It gave details of the raids, with the headline 'Nationwide security police raids: 104 raided – 9 known to be held'. The newsletter included this anonymous poem, entitled 'Sunday':

> I am 5.00 am
> I am a knock on your front door
> I am two men from the political police
> I am a warrant to try and accuse
> I am an order to ban or detain
>
> I am 5.00 am
> I am searching your bedroom
> I am reading your books, your letters, your diary
> I am retrieving the carnation
> Yesterday crumpled in your wastepaper basket
>
> I am 5.00 am
> I am the hidden precipice of unknown
> I am the invisible fear
> whispering in the back of your mind:
> I have come to take you away[21]

A few days after the raids I received a letter from an Anglican priest, Charles Parry, who knew me and my family well. He had for some years been our parish priest in the farming district where I grew up. He wrote:

I have little idea how you may be feeling about having the SB going through your room – which I read about in the paper this morning – because nothing like this has ever happened to me. If it did though, I would not enjoy it. I read *NUX* quite frequently, and if that is the reason you attracted their attention, you have nothing to be ashamed of. It is a far more interesting, readable and alive paper than what circulated in Maritzburg while I was there. Most of all it has a conscience and tries to arouse the consciences of the students. Such a contribution is sorely needed among the mass of students, and in South Africa generally, and for that reason I don't believe you will allow yourself to bow to their intimidation.[22]

What does it feel like when the security police come for you at 4.00 am on a Sunday morning? What does this do to you, deep inside? I still don't know the answer, but it certainly scared me. And I had final exams in just a couple of weeks. As it happened, I failed two of my four subjects and could not complete my degree. I had tasted the struggle for justice and truth, and I had paid a price. But it was not nearly as severe a price as that paid by many others that I knew and counted as friends and fellow Christians. I also knew that I was staring into very deep water. Next time it was unlikely that I would get away so lightly.

5

In the wilderness

After I had finished my final exams at the University of Natal, I went home to the farm. Although I still had two credits to complete to gain my degree, I needed to get away. I decided to move to Johannesburg, far from all that had happened over the past three years. I took a job working as a clerk in the Johannesburg traffic court, and lived for a while at the YMCA. I was adrift. The city of Johannesburg seemed like a good place to hide, to wait and see what the next step might be.

Weeks later I went back to the farm for a few nights. My bedroom was in a small outbuilding close to the main house. I was fast asleep one night when, in the middle of the night, there was a loud banging on my door. 'Maak oop, Meneer Cowley! Dit is die securiteitse polisie!' came the shout from outside my door – 'Open up! This is the security police!' My heart sank. I could not believe it. They've come for me here, I thought. Even here, on the farm miles from anywhere, where I thought I was safe, even here they had found me.

I opened the door in dread and despair. There stood my cousin and a friend of his, both students at Natal University. They were driving back from what was then Rhodesia (now Zimbabwe) and were passing the farm in the middle of the night. They had decided to stop and wake me up for a bit of a laugh. What a relief! I could have wept with joy. But I have never forgotten that awful, sinking feeling.

In Johannesburg I took the opportunity to explore new interests and aspects of life. There was no pressure, and in the big city I could be anonymous. I attended a creative writing course at Wits University, went to concerts and movies, and worked for a while in a record shop in Hillbrow, a vibrant cosmopolitan area with cinemas, bookshops and restaurants. The only church I visited during this time was a place called the Miracle Centre. This was a Pentecostal group that met in the basement of a building near Hillbrow. There was no liturgy or sacrament, but there was fiery preaching and lots of loud singing, and the main focus was prayer for miracles and healing. Somehow I thought I might find God there. They seemed to know something about a powerful, supernatural God which I longed to experience for myself.

After six months in Johannesburg it was time for me to return to Natal to complete the outstanding courses for my degree. I arranged to live in one of the university residences for a few months while I prepared to rewrite the examinations. Here I met a group of young men who enjoyed spending time most days visiting bars and pubs in the wider Pietermaritzburg area. We would work until 8.00 pm and then pile into Harry's car and head off to the Imperial or the Ansonia, the Hilton or the Camelot. We drank beer, and we usually got back to the residence around midnight. There was no need to get up early in the mornings. I felt as if my life was on hold, going nowhere until I passed my degree. What the future would hold for me, I had no idea.

After the examinations were finished, four of us decided to end our university careers on a high. We drove to the port city of Durban for a big celebration. We went from one bar to another, and eventually were picked up by the police as we staggered down the street singing and shouting. We were bundled into the back of a police van and driven around for a couple of hours. I didn't care. This was nothing compared to what I had been through before. Eventually the police let us go and told us to go home and not cause any more trouble.

The turning point

A few days later I set off with another friend from the residence, Peter Southey, to spend a week at a work camp in a remote rural part of South Africa at Kentani in the Transkei. Pete Southey was a Christian, and the camp was organised by the Students' Christian

Association (SCA), a conservative, Bible-centred group working in the white English-speaking universities. SCA was not a group that I was comfortable with, but I was drawn to the idea of doing some hard manual work building a classroom at a remote mission station in a beautiful part of South Africa.

The missionary at Kentani was a man named Harry Oosthuizen. He and his wife and family lived very simply, by faith in Jesus. In the living room of their house was a large sign with the words in Afrikaans, 'gebed verander omstandighede' – 'prayer changes circumstances'. The first night we were there, I became aware that there was a problem in the kitchen. There were about 50 or 60 students, who had arrived from different universities around the country. The only food that the Oosthuizens had to feed us, apart from vegetables, was one chicken and a tin of stew. 'How is this going to feed us all?' someone asked. But it all went into a big pot, and amazingly there was enough for everyone. I started to think that there was something going on here that I had never seen before.

As the days passed, I knew more and more clearly that what I was encountering here, in a way that I had never previously known, was the presence of Jesus. I was deeply struck by the kindness and humility and devotion to Jesus that I saw in 'Uncle Harry' and his wife. They lived very simply, and they had an obvious and extraordinary love and care for the people around them. I came to realise that it is one thing to believe in God and in Christianity, but it is another altogether to love Jesus with all our hearts and to surrender our lives to him. Here, in this place so far away from the bustle of normal life, I could see very clearly a quality of truth and love that I had not encountered before.

I was faced with a dawning realisation that Jesus Christ is truly 'God with us', Emmanuel. If this is true, completely true, and he died for me, then this changes everything. It seemed to me to be a question of truth. I could see in the lives of the people around me, and as I read the Bible with new eyes, that here I had somehow stumbled upon the truth. I could not simply go away and continue my life as before.

So one Friday morning, in December 1972, I walked out alone to a scruffy mealie (maize) field, sat down and very deliberately counted the cost and surrendered my will and every area of my life to the Lord Jesus Christ. At that point my life changed irrevocably and forever.

I went back home, and I knew that I was different. From now on I was going to be publicly and openly a Christian, committed to living as a disciple of Jesus and to telling others about him. I discovered, for the first time, the reality of the power of the Holy Spirit in my personal experience. These were the early days of what became known as the worldwide charismatic renewal. When I returned to Pietermaritzburg in the new year, I met a number of Christian students who spoke of being 'zapped' by the Holy Spirit. This was something new and extraordinary: a personal experience of being filled to overflowing with the love and joy and power of God. It wasn't just me. This surrender to Jesus and empowering by the Spirit of God was happening in the lives of many people that I knew. Lives were being changed by the power and love of God in Jesus Christ.

Christian revival in South Africa

I threw myself into this new way of living with total commitment and unflinching boldness. There were still awful things happening in South Africa, but now somehow there seemed to be hope. 'If God is at work, then surely anything is possible,' I said. In March 1973 a group of NUSAS leaders were given five-year banning orders by the government. I was appalled and angry. What could I do? At that point, I felt, all that I could do was to give myself wholly to being the person that God had called me to be, and trust him to work in me and in others whom he was calling to bring about change and a new South Africa. I would seek first the kingdom of God and his righteousness, and trust him for everything else.

I had now completed my degree and begun working in the Natal Registry of Deeds in Pietermaritzburg. My plan had been to pursue a career in law, so I continued studying part-time, although I could sense that my priorities in life were changing rapidly. I continued to write for *NUX*. In April 1973, in an article entitled 'Christian revival in South Africa', I wrote:

> Over the past year or so, something of a Christian revival has started in South Africa. In Cape Town and Johannesburg, in Grahamstown and now even in Maritzburg, Christianity has been making a new impact on the lives of South Africans. A God-filled revival is something difficult to define or even to visualise. They have happened in the past, although there are very few people who have actually lived through one.
>
> One cannot plan for revival; it is difficult enough to be aware of it when it does happen. Nonetheless, something unusual is happening here. Many people who have considered themselves Christians of one sort or another, as well as those with no religious affiliations at all, have felt this and have been forced to start wondering what is happening.
>
> Certainly, if there was ever a need for a Christian revival, that need is in South Africa at this time. Not only is the church a tragically ineffective organisation, but our society is more rotten with hatred and injustice than ever before. The future, as every white liberal knows, is a sad and virtually hopeless picture. Now, almost suddenly, the intervention of God in the South African situation has become an alternative as a possible solution to its problems.[23]

In Pietermaritzburg, a small Christian evangelistic organisation called Africa Enterprise had set up an office above one of the local banks. Africa Enterprise was led by Michael Cassidy, who had a vision of bringing the South African churches together in the work of mission and evangelism. In March 1973 Africa Enterprise organised a large multiracial conference in Durban called the South African Congress on Mission and Evangelism. Billy Graham came to Durban to address the congress and to preach at an evangelistic rally at the King's Park rugby stadium in Durban. I trained as a counsellor for the Billy Graham rally and attended both the rally and some of the congress. This was a new kind of Christianity. It was Christ-centred, biblical and evangelistic, and it was also multiracial, intellectually rigorous and fully engaged with the world. I couldn't help but be drawn into the energy and vision which Michael Cassidy and his fellow leaders, black and white, seemed to bring to our polarised and broken society.

During my time in UCM, the institutional church had increasingly seemed out of touch, resistant to change and complicit in supporting and maintaining the present political system. Now I started to see a vision of a church that looked much more like the church of the New Testament. To my amazement even the Anglican church was starting to reclaim some of the joy and abundant life which I read about in the book of Acts:

> Awe came upon everyone, because many wonders and signs were being done by the apostles. All who believed were together and had all things in common; they would sell their possessions and goods and distribute the proceeds to all, as any had need. Day by day, as they spent much time together in the temple, they broke bread at home and ate their food with glad and generous hearts, praising God and having the goodwill of all the people. And day by day the Lord added to their number those who were being saved.
> ACTS 2:43–47

This was the kind of community that I began to see coming into being around me. We believed in an alternative society, a new way of living based on radical discipleship and abandonment of our lives to Jesus. This was our hope for the future of our country.

I was filled with zealous enthusiasm for my new-found faith in Christ. But behind this smiling face lurked pain and a deep concern for a country that, humanly speaking, was heading for disaster. It seems to me now that I had come to this point of commitment to Christ through an utter desperation to find something that made sense of all that I had been through. My experience in UCM, and what I had seen happening to others around me, had left me numb and broken. So what I did, as I see it now, was to throw myself into God, as I best understood how to do this. I devoured the Bible and gave myself wholeheartedly to the Christian fellowship on the campus. These were now my brothers and sisters in Christ. My discovery of the love of God for me in Christ Jesus seemed to be the way forward: a way to make sense of all that had happened to me in those previous years.

I do not believe that this was escapism. This was about turning to God in a hopeless situation and believing that if God is love then he alone is the ultimate solution to all our needs. This meant surrendering my life to Jesus and finding my peace in God's unfailing mercy and love. Then I would be enabled to go out and live a life of ever-deeper obedience to him. I knew that I was not alone in this. I was surrounded by others whom God was calling, as he was calling me. Together we would become a new community who were all one in Christ Jesus, a people of hope in a broken world.

6

The fire of love

In 1974 my hunger for God led me to the Penguin Classics series of books on Christian spirituality. I bought and read *The Imitation of Christ* by Thomas à Kempis. This was strong meat for a young Christian. I was drawn to his 'Counsels on the Inner Life', with their emphasis on self-denial, the renunciation of worldly interests and pursuits and the surrender of all other loves before the love of Jesus. I bought and read Gerald Vann's spiritual classic *The Divine Pity: A study in the social implications of the beatitudes*. Then I discovered *The Fire of Love* by Richard Rolle.

Richard Rolle was a medieval hermit and mystic, born around the year 1300 at Thornton-le-Dale in Yorkshire. On the back cover of the Penguin Classic edition of *The Fire of Love* I read:

> Richard Rolle's *The Fire of Love* burns with the flame of a medieval mystic's love of God. Here he proves for others the joy he feels, alone in the unutterable knowledge of his Creator. His treatise is partly autobiographical and partly a practical manual to the devout life. Erratic, even turbulent at times, *The Fire of Love* explores the shadow-land beyond the realm of common Christian experience.[24]

These words went straight to my heart. This was now my own desire. I wanted more than anything to be on fire for God, to know more of his joy, more of his power, more of his infinite love. I longed to give everything for this 'unutterable knowledge of my Creator'. What could be more valuable, more important in life, more thrilling and ultimately more significant than to know God and lose myself in the fire of his love? I had seen the pearl of great price which, Jesus says, is the kingdom of heaven (Matthew 13:45–46), and more than anything else this was what I desired for myself.

Richard Rolle is, like Thomas à Kempis, not normally the kind of reading that you would recommend to a young Christian. This is uncompromising mystical Christian discipleship, which emphasises not only the consistent practice of righteousness but also the 'filthiness of soft living' and the longing of the whole heart for the perfect love of God. What seemed particularly important to me about Richard Rolle was his insight that to be drawn to God was to be drawn to the fire of his unquenchable love. This is all about love. To know God is to know love in its purest and most exalted form. This was why I had turned to God in the crisis and tragedy of what was happening around me. When the world is falling apart, where do we turn for hope and meaning? Surely it is love that is the enduring and eternal answer to our plight and trouble. Richard Rolle says:

> The splendour of our reward depends on the greatness of our love, and the one who loves very greatly burns with an unquenchable blaze, and is filled with heavenly sweetness. The more generous his love, the higher his standing in the Kingdom...
>
> Nothing is better than mutual love, nothing sweeter than holy charity. To love and be loved is the delightful purpose of all human life; the delight of angels and of God, and the reward of blessedness. If then you want to be loved, love! Love gets love in return. No one has ever lost through loving good, if he has persisted in love to the end.[25]

I longed to give myself completely to God, and to live my life for him in the service of his redeeming love. As well as reading Rolle and Kempis, I attended evangelical Christian weekend camps and discipleship training courses. A lot of this was about discipleship and prayer and witnessing to Jesus Christ in our words and our lives. There was a strong emphasis on the need to get up early in the morning to pray and listen to God and read the Bible. We were also taught to avoid steady relationships with the opposite sex unless it was clearly 'God's time'. We were told that we should not get serious with anyone unless we were ready for marriage.

Looking back at my journals from this time, it seems to me now that I was quite hard on myself. I kept a daily prayer journal in which I wrote: 'I must use every minute of my time for work and for God. No waste'; 'What I need is a greater self-discipline'; 'Obedience is essential. You cannot please yourself if you want to please God.'

I was hard on others too. In 1973 I had met a girl who was studying the same course at university as me. She seemed to like me, and we began to spend time together. She introduced me to Schubert and Mozart and to bicycle trips with a picnic basket in the countryside. She was Roman Catholic, but not as strongly committed as I was to following Jesus above all else. The teaching that I was receiving was that young men should not get involved romantically with young women, especially if they were not committed to Jesus. So I agonised and I prayed, and eventually I took her out for a drive. I told her that we could not continue this relationship and I was not going to see her one-to-one any more. She was sad and upset and didn't really understand. She fought back her tears as I took her back and left her at the university residence. I wish that I could somehow tell her that I am sorry. But it is too late for that now.

So my pursuit of the fire of God's love may have been zealous and highly committed, but I was not always kind or compassionate, to others or even myself. I still had a lot to learn about the true nature of the love of God. A good Christian friend at university tried to help me see that serving God did not have to be so serious and intense. She pointed me to Jesus saying that he had come that we might have life and have it abundantly (John 10:10). She told me that we should be able to enjoy all good things in God, that his love is life-giving and life-affirming and that his purpose is not to make us hard and judgemental. So I wrote this down in my notebook too.

In all of this I was caught up in an extraordinary sense of God at work, in me and in others around me, through the power of the Holy Spirit. Unquestionably I knew that my life had been changed by Jesus Christ, and I could see the same thing happening to other young people, mainly fellow students.

As mentioned in the previous chapter, this was a time when charismatic renewal hit the church, and experiences that had been common in Pentecostal churches broke through into the life of the mainline denominations. Worship was transformed from something dry and dull to a joy-filled exuberant celebration of the power of God at work in his people. We expected to see God at work, changing lives, healing people, transforming the church. Surely the transformation of our society could not be far behind, because with God nothing is impossible.

We were filled with a new passion for Jesus and an all-consuming desire to make the love of Jesus known to others. Reading the Bible was not an effort, but a joy, as truth seemed to leap out at me from page after page. Getting up early to praise and worship God, to pray and to listen to his word was central to my life. This was the passion of first love.

It seems inevitable that this early fervour and excitement in knowing and serving Jesus does not continue unchanged as we travel through life. The Psalms speak of the times when we cry out to God because he seems far off and our prayers seem as though they are not being answered – 'Why, O Lord, do you stand far off? Why do you hide yourself in times of trouble?' (Psalm 10:1). I can see now that this is all part of the life of faith, where sometimes God seems extraordinarily close and real, but at other times we simply have to persevere in the deep commitment of our lives.

Finding my vocation

Richard Rolle says that the contemplative heart is a heart which is on fire with the love of God and which is ruled by love. To be contemplative is to give yourself to God and to the fire of his love. Rolle writes:

> The more ardent a man's love, the more exalted his reward. For there is in true contemplatives a certain sweet fervour and an abundance of God's love, which because it abides in them infuses them with joy and song, and ineffable pleasure.[26]

In this vision of a life fully yielded to God and to his redeeming love in Jesus, I had, I knew, found my life's calling and purpose. My vocation was to give my life to the service and ministry of Jesus. But what kind of ministry was I being called to? Early in October 1974, I was elected president of the local branch of the Anglican Students' Federation (ASF). I was increasingly impressed by the ASF, which was led by ordained Anglican chaplains such as Livingstone Ngewu, Rob Perks and Ivan Weiss. Here I encountered a vision for the church which was dramatically different from the Anglican church I had grown up in. The ASF had remained committed to holding together students of all races in one organisation, despite the increasing pressure from black consciousness. Father Sigqibo Dwane from the Federal Theological Seminary, in an address to the ASF, spoke of the need to find a way to bridge the cultural and racial divisions of our society. Ian M. Macqueen writes:

> In a similar way to the manner in which the early church had overcome the division between Jew and Gentile, Dwane sought to remind his audience that 'black and white Christians must also find time to look at each other and talk and do things together'. For the very reason that there was 'so much pressure from white society and certain elements in black consciousness to separate', it was imperative for 'young Christians to meet and remind one another about the Gospel and the true nature of the Church'. This meeting gave a new meaning to liberation,

whereby blacks could liberate whites from suspicion and fear, and blacks could be liberated from 'obsequiousness and feelings of inferiority'.[27]

I found myself drawn to the blend of youthful dynamism, radical Christianity and liturgical depth which I experienced at ASF gatherings. The ASF seemed to bring together the key strands of my own journey. To my surprise, I was being drawn back into the Anglican church.

Through Ivan Weiss, the chaplain at Rhodes University, I was introduced to Bill Burnett, who was then the bishop of Grahamstown and was soon to become archbishop of Cape Town. In January 1974 I travelled down to Grahamstown to meet Bishop Bill and to discuss my future in the church. I had discussed with Ivan Weiss the possibility of working for the bishop among students and young people in Grahamstown for a year. I stayed with Bill Burnett in Kenton-on-Sea, on the eastern Cape coast. Bishop Bill took me for a long walk along the beach from Kenton to the Diaz cross, past the vast sand dunes, picking up cowrie shells as the waves from the Indian Ocean crashed down on the shore. He listened to me carefully and pointed me in a new direction. Within a few months my life's course had been settled. I had been accepted as an Anglican ordinand and was preparing to go to England to train for full-time ministry for the Anglican church.

Going forward into ordained ministry in the church in South Africa seemed to be the way in which I could take forward all that I had learnt and experienced in my time with UCM, as well as fulfilling my desire to know and serve God. A number of other students that I had met in UCM followed this path into ordained ministry and were able to make their contribution to the transformation of South Africa through the life and witness of the churches. But for others who had been part of UCM this was never going to be an option. Some left the country and put UCM behind them; others simply got on with their lives and continued to work as best they could for justice and change. Other students that I knew took a different and more radical, and often far more costly, path.

Rick Turner was a senior lecturer in political science at the University of Natal in the 1970s. In 1972 he wrote a study entitled *The Eye of the Needle* for the Special Programme for Christian Action in Society, published by the Christian Institute in South Africa. Turner was a very influential figure among radical white students in South Africa in the early 1970s. He himself had become increasingly influenced by Steve Biko and the black consciousness movement. In *The Eye of the Needle*, Turner wrote:

> When asking what sort of society is compatible with Christianity, we have first to ask whether Christianity embodies an internal morality or a transcendent morality. And the answer is obvious. The essence of all religions lies in the concept of transcendence, that is, in the idea of something (whether it be a 'reality' or an 'ideal') which goes beyond the present, which goes beyond what people are doing in the world at this moment, and in the light of which the present is only of secondary importance. Religion challenges the common-sense tendency to be committed to the present, to see the world as we experience it now as the only possible form of reality. This challenge occurs on two inter-related levels: in terms of a transcendent reality (God); and in terms of a transcendent ethic.[28]

Turner says that 'for Christianity, what I should be is defined by the example of Jesus Christ'. He goes on to argue that what he calls the 'Christian human model' of living in society is very different from the capitalist model: 'If I concentrate on things, rather than people, I become a slave. I become dependent on things.' He then sets out to construct a model for society that in his understanding would be 'compatible with Christianity and free of destructive conflict'.[29]

Turner looked at how a deeply divided South African society might possibly be able to change peacefully into a participatory democracy. He recognised the importance of economic development and the key role of black workers for the future of the South African economy. He felt that the bargaining power of black workers in formal and informal

worker organisations and trades unions would be of central importance in bringing about significant social and political change in South
Africa.

On Monday 9 January 1978, I was travelling through Johannesburg
airport on my way to London, when I read in a newspaper that Turner
had been shot dead in his kitchen in Durban on Sunday morning. He
died in the arms of his 13-year-old daughter. No one has ever been
arrested or found guilty of his murder.

A number of students that I knew were influenced by Turner's
ideas and became increasingly involved in the black trades union
movement. Among these was Pat Horn, whom I had met at the UCM
conference in 1970 and visited a number of times when she was at
Wits University.

Horn had failed to complete her degree because of her involvement
in student politics. She had received a five-year banning order and
devoted her life to organising and supporting unskilled workers in
the informal economy. In 1993 she was instrumental in setting up
the Self-Employed Women's Union, which negotiated with municipal
authorities on behalf of street vendors in major urban areas across
South Africa to provide better facilities such as toilets, water, shelter,
safety and child day-care centres. Horn also organised informal
workers at the international level through setting up StreetNet International, which has 52 affiliates in 46 countries.

In 2016 I read in the University of KwaZulu-Natal magazine that Pat
Horn had been awarded an honorary doctorate by my old university,
'in recognition of her distinguished service and significant contribution
to improving the fabric of South African society.'[30] In her address to
graduates she spoke of the responsibility each person has to listen to
and to support the most marginalised in society:

> When you are that civil servant working in a local or national gov-
> ernment department, don't be the arrogant one who looks down

on informal workers because you think they are uneducated –
be the one who sees in front of you human beings with dignity,
family and community responsibilities. Put yourself in the shoes
of those you are employed to serve, in order to understand
better and serve people more effectively.[31]

Pat Horn's vocation has been very different from mine, and yet both
of our vocations were formed through our time in the University
Christian Movement. Through UCM we were given the ideal of a life
given to serve others, especially the poor, and to work, sometimes
at great cost, for justice and the transformation of society. To serve
a transcendent God requires of us a transcendent ethic. If we know
God and the fire of Christlike love, we will not accept a world which is
rooted and grounded in anything less than the values and example of
Jesus. This is the heart of the contemplative struggle.

Part Two

The eye of the needle: action and contemplation

Again I tell you, it is easier for a camel to go through the eye of a needle than for someone who is rich to enter the kingdom of God.

MATTHEW 19:24

7

Christ in you, the hope of glory

In your inner self Christ has made his home.
St Augustine of Hippo

In Colossians 1:27 we find this extraordinary phrase: 'Christ in you, the hope of glory.' Our hope for the future, our hope of knowing and sharing in the glory of God now and in all eternity is this: Christ in you and Christ in me.

What does this mean, that Jesus is in me and in you? It means that he is here, he is living in my inner being, in the deepest and truest part of who I am. Jesus has come to live in me, 24/7. Jesus, the one who says, 'I am the way, and the truth, and the life' (John 14:6), has come to us and made his home in us. My whole future, my hope of glory, lies in knowing this great mystery and truth of the Christian faith, which is Christ in me, and then living accordingly.

We live in an age when vast amounts of personal information are being harvested and stored by internet companies. These are used to direct our shopping preferences and internet searches, form our attitudes and change our habits. We may even find our conversations listened to by devices in our homes and in our pockets. This kind of continuous surveillance is not what is meant by 'Christ in you, the hope of glory'. We are not being watched and controlled by some remote internet giant or intelligence agency. But 'Christ in you' is the presence within us of Jesus himself; he is with me always (Matthew 28:20). But more than that, he is in me. He knows my thoughts, my attitudes, my motives. Nothing is hidden from him. He knows everything about me, and still he loves me. He is in me as my friend, my redeemer and my Lord.

A contemplative heart is a heart which is ruled by the presence of Christ in us – by his love and his peace. As Christians we yield our hearts and lives to Christ in us, because we know and believe that he is trustworthy and that he cares for us. We know that his way, the way of Jesus, is the way of perfect love.

Abide in me

John 15 begins with Jesus' great teaching about the vine and the branches: 'I am the true vine, and my Father is the vine-grower.' In verse 4 Jesus says, 'Abide in me as I abide in you.' Jesus goes on to say, 'I am the vine, you are the branches. Those who abide in me and I in them bear much fruit, because apart from me you can do nothing' (v. 5). Again we see this extraordinary truth which even practising Christians may often miss or overlook. It is simply this: Christ is in us. He has made his home in our hearts; he abides in us, and he tells us that we too must abide in him.

The word 'abide' is not often used in everyday speech these days. The Greek word *menó* means to stay, to remain, to be present or to dwell. The word is used many times in the New Testament. Christians are exhorted to abide or remain in the Lord in order to be rooted in him, to be knit to him by the Spirit, whom they received from him (see 1 John 2:6, 24, 27; 3:6). To abide is to maintain unbroken fellowship with someone, to be loyal and to endure. The word can also mean to stay in someone's house or to live in a certain town or country.

To abide in Christ means to dwell or live in him and become more and more like him. His promise to us is that he also lives in us. So the apostle Paul is able to speak of 'the mystery that has been hidden throughout the ages and generations but has now been revealed to his saints. To them God chose to make known how great among the Gentiles are the riches of the glory of this mystery, which is Christ in you, the hope of glory' (Colossians 1:26–27).

It is important to see that, as Paul says, we are talking about a mystery. There are many things at the heart of the life of faith which we can never fully comprehend with our finite human minds. These are the deep things of God, the holy mysteries, where we, like Moses, need to simply take off our shoes and bow down and worship, because we are standing on holy ground. To enter such mysteries, we need more than intellect. We open our hearts to God and to his love, and for this we need to move beyond words and into silence.

God has come to us in his Son, Jesus, and has made his home in our hearts by the Holy Spirit. He abides in us. He lives in us. And we are called, therefore, to abide in him and to live according to his law of love. This brings about a radical transformation of our whole way of being. We live no longer for ourselves and our own interests. Instead, we now live a Christ-centred life. We give our lives in love for God, for others and for the world. Paul spells this out:

> I have been crucified with Christ; and it is no longer I who live, but it is Christ who lives in me. And the life I now live in the flesh I live by faith in the Son of God, who loved me and gave himself for me.
> GALATIANS 2:19–20

There is a principle at work here, which is that if Christ is to live in me, then my old 'me-first' self has to die. To live a life of love is to live no longer for ourselves, but for others and for God. This is why Paul says that 'it is no longer I who live, but it is Christ who lives in me'. This is a radical departure from the individualistic view of life that has developed rapidly since the mid-20th century across much of the western world. We live in a world of me, me, me. But the way of love that is revealed in Jesus is a radically different way of living.

A contemplative heart is one that is rooted and held firm in the love of Jesus. In John 15:9 Jesus says, 'As the Father has loved me, so I have loved you; abide in my love.' His is the voice of love, deep within. When we surrender ourselves to Christ, we put to death the old, egocentric false self, and we live by faith in the Son of God. Then I become my true self in Christ, as I find that my life 'is hidden with Christ in God' (Colossians 3:3). Our whole world view is transformed, so that we may come to see others as Jesus sees them, and we see our world as Jesus sees it. All our behaviour patterns, attitudes and desires will be affected and changed. Nothing is excluded.

This is the true meaning of conversion. Conversion to Christ is not, as is sometimes portrayed, merely a ticket to eternal life through believing in Jesus. It is that, but it is so much more. Conversion to Christ is a fundamentally changed way of living. It is Christ in us, ruling our hearts, our words, our actions, our lives.

This does not happen overnight. It is a journey, in which day by day we need grace and the unfailing compassion of God. This is a process of inner transformation, of learning to see things differently. We may find that this requires significant intentional inner work, and we may need the help of others who understand the journey we are on and who are able to support and guide us. We offer up our hearts and our lives, and we are led by the Holy Spirit and changed each day, more and more, into the likeness of Jesus. The work of the Spirit of God in our hearts can be a painful journey into greater self-knowledge and integrity. We are all a work in progress. What matters is not the finished article but the direction of travel.

The contemplative heart seeks each day to be attentive and obedient to the whispers and promptings of the Lord. We are not yet what we will become, but we are on the way. The inner transformation of Christ in us will need to reach a deeper level than can ever be achieved by the sheer exercise of will. This involves a significant work of the Holy Spirit, and a yielding, a letting go, in which the practice of contemplative prayer can be enormously helpful. Here we are held firm in our inmost being by the presence of the Lord with us, the inner voice of love. This is the great mystery, which is Christ in us, the hope of glory.

8

A war of desires

In his letter to the Galatians, the apostle Paul spells out the radically transformed way of living that flows from knowing Christ in us, the hope of glory. He says, 'Live by the Spirit, I say, and do not gratify the desires of the flesh. For what the flesh desires is opposed to the Spirit, and what the Spirit desires is opposed to the flesh' (Galatians 5:16–17). To live by the Spirit is to live a Christ-centred life. If our hearts are ruled by the presence of Christ in us, we will be drawn by his Spirit away from the need to gratify the desires of the flesh, the 'me-first' false self.

This is a key issue for disciples of Jesus in our distracted 21st-century culture. I was talking to my son about this, and he recommended I listen to a series of podcasts from KXC (King's Cross Church) in London, based on their teaching series 'War of desires'. KXC was planted from St Mary's Church in Bryanston Square in 2010 and has a large congregation of mainly young adults. The series aimed to address some of the issues young adults are struggling with, particularly in places like London. They say that 'misdirected loves lead to misdirected lives'. They then look at the pursuit of comfort, self-sufficiency, entitlement and status and the problem of shame, and explore what it means to 'love Jesus above all else'.[32]

To live by the Spirit means to love Jesus above all else and to live according to his will and character. To live by the flesh means to live for ourselves, with self at the centre. The Greek word which is usually translated as 'flesh' is *sarx*. *Sarx* is a difficult word for us to understand, as it cannot be translated directly into English: it 'may simply mean the body' or 'the sphere of birth and natural descent'.[33] The word can be used in a number of different ways. It may be used for observable, external things as opposed to spiritual things, or even for the whole sphere of imperfection and sinfulness. It is important to grasp that, in principle, *sarx* (or flesh) is morally neutral. It is part of the way God has made us. But the flesh is weak, and there is 'a dynamic hostility between flesh and spirit, set out in Galatians 5:16–23, and more fully in Romans 8:3–14'.[34]

The flesh is egocentric. It is concerned with self-preservation, self-promotion and self-interest, about how I appear to other people and what they may or may not be thinking of me. The flesh is the 'me-first' self, which prioritises my needs and my interests over those of others and is preoccupied with protecting and defending my own 'safe world', my material possessions, security and reputation. This is the world where the individual matters far more than the wider community.

Much of our 21st-century culture is geared towards reinforcing this view of life. We are brought up, from an early age, to define our identity as individuals by our own interests and preferences and by our physical space. Even as children, we often have our own bedrooms, with our posters on the wall and our own stuff scattered around us. We feel we have the right to defend and protect what we see as our space. I am aware of my own reaction sometimes when someone is imposing themselves into the space where I want to be comfortable, perhaps in a coffee shop or restaurant or when I am driving. 'You are impinging on my space' is my own inner reaction, as though the world belongs to me, and I have the right not to be bothered or upset by other people and their lives. When self-interest is uppermost in our hearts, generosity, patience and gentleness are the losers.

This is the age of the individual. I am conditioned by my culture to constantly assert and protect my personal right, as I perceive it, to live my life in my own way and for my own pleasure and self-fulfilment. Previous generations understood the importance of a sense of duty: the duty which is bestowed upon us as human persons to give ourselves to service, family and community and to work for the greater good of society. In the age of the selfie, this view of life is squeezed to the margins.

The true self and the false self

Thomas Merton, the great teacher and writer on spirituality and prayer, says that the true self is the person God made me to be and is calling me to become in Christ. Merton writes: 'Our vocation is not simply to be, but to work together with God in the creation of our own life, our own identity, our own destiny.'[35] Merton also writes about the false self, which is essentially the flesh as the New Testament understands it. This is the egocentric, 'me-first' self, which sees life not as centred on God and on his purposes for us and our world, but on ourselves. To live by the Spirit is to become our true selves in Christ. If instead we live to gratify the desires of the flesh, we are false selves, who have chosen to live with our hearts set not on God but on ourselves. There is then a profound dislocation at the centre of our being.

God is love, and his purposes are entirely loving, just and good. The pursuit and protection of narrow self-interest for myself or 'my group' leads directly to greed, resentment, conflict and exploitation of others. The ways of the Lord are peace, joy, reconciliation, patience, long-suffering, gentleness and self-control. The ways of the flesh may promise security and pleasure, but they never bring lasting peace, satisfaction or contentment. They set us in competition against one another and against God, and this always leads to trouble.

As we look at the world around us now, we see everywhere the rotten fruit of this way of being and living. The planet is burning, and the waters are rising. Global inequality of wealth and income daily grows more stark and serious. Professional footballers in Britain earn £500,000 per week, while across Africa millions live on less than a pound a day. We spend billions on armaments, and we know that a nuclear catastrophe could be just around the corner. Our lives seem to be ever more frantic, as digital devices and social media dominate our every waking hour. We desperately need to find again 'the things that make for peace', as Jesus said as he wept over Jerusalem (Luke 19:42).

For Merton, 'The only true joy on earth is to escape from the prisons of our own false self, and enter by love into union with the Life who dwells and sings within the essence of every creature and in the core of our own souls.'[36] This is what it means to become my true self.

When our lives are directed by the false self, we are living lives of sin. We make ourselves the rulers of creation, and then we may even choose to say, 'Of course there is no creator; there is no God.' This is nothing new, despite the recent rise of 'new atheism'; it is as old as human history. In Psalm 14:1, written more than 2,500 years ago, we read, 'Fools say in their hearts, "There is no God."'

Our lives are in God's hands. The whole Bible, and the experience of millions upon millions of people of faith through the ages, tells us that this is the ultimate truth of our life on this earth. Above all, the life and teaching of Jesus Christ reveal to us the love of God our Father and creator. Jesus himself lived on earth a life of perfect love and perfect truth, unlike any other life in the whole of human history. Jesus is utterly unique, in his life, his death and his resurrection. If we are to find a way of hope and healing in these tumultuous times, we must return to the ultimate reality of who we are and what our lives are for.

Contemplation: learn contemplative practice

Why is it that we find ourselves longing for all that God promises us, and yet pursuing endlessly those things which only bring more trouble and strife to our lives and to our world?

We are all caught up in the 'war of desires'. This is the struggle between the true self and the false self, between the call to live by the Spirit and the temptation to gratify the desires of the flesh. There is no easy answer or quick solution here. We live each day making choices. Sometimes we make good choices, and we see the fruit of those. But sometimes we do not. Like Paul we can say:

> I delight in the law of God in my inmost self, but I see in my
> members another law at war with the law of my mind, making
> me captive to the law of sin that dwells in my members.
> Wretched man that I am! Who will rescue me from this body of
> death? Thanks be to God through Jesus Christ our Lord!
> ROMANS 7:22–25

What I have found, in my own searching and struggling, is that the
more I continue in daily contemplative practice, the more my heart
is enabled to be ruled and held firm by the peace of God in Christ
Jesus. The more that I do this, being still in the presence of God for a
set period of time each day, the more I find that God is able, in some
mysterious way, to change my heart and draw me to himself. Like
Paul, we can say:

This, too, is nothing new. Contemplative prayer is something that has
been known and taught as essential to true Christian prayer since the
early days of the Christian church. Many of the early church fathers of
the first three centuries were contemplatives who were practised in
silent prayer and solitude, and who taught this as an essential part of
true discipleship. This remains as vitally important today as it has ever
been. In fact, it may be that contemplative practice has become an
essential discipline for those who are seeking to be faithful disciples
of Christ in the 21st century. Rowan Williams, the former archbishop
of Canterbury, writes:

> Contemplation is very far from being just one kind of thing
> that Christians do: it is the key to prayer, liturgy, art and ethics,
> the key to the essence of a renewed humanity that is capable
> of seeing the world and other subjects in the world with
> freedom – freedom from self-oriented, acquisitive habits and
> the distorted understanding that comes from these. To put it
> boldly, contemplation is the only ultimate answer to the unreal
> and insane world that our financial systems and our advertising
> culture and our chaotic and unexamined emotions encourage us
> to inhabit. To learn contemplative practice is to learn what we

need to live truthfully and honestly and lovingly. It is a deeply revolutionary matter.[37]

What does it mean to know and follow Jesus Christ in the 'unreal and insane world that our financial systems and our advertising culture and our chaotic and unexamined emotions encourage us to inhabit'?

The culture of consumerism and self-fulfilment is everywhere around us. It is the air we breathe, the water in which we swim. Many of our fundamental assumptions about who we are and what life is about are now formed by a particular form of capitalism that is relentlessly focused on the desires of the consumer. It is hard to see the wood for the trees, to see the truth that brings peace for the bright and beautiful images with which we are bombarded every day. To return to a life of simple obedience to the teachings and practice of Jesus Christ is immensely challenging. Is this even possible?

All of this takes me back to South Africa in the early 1970s, when those of us who were seen as white Christian liberals in UCM tried to wrestle with the challenge of living with integrity in apartheid South Africa. We were talking about some kind of 'white consciousness' which would enable us to live faithfully and truthfully in a society that opposed the ways of Jesus so powerfully and subtly. Our lives were inextricably linked with this alien ideology and culture. Could there be a third way, one that did not involve either collusion with the system or exile and escape?

This seems to me to be much the same dilemma that many are struggling with in our own times. We see young people, many in their teens and early 20s, showing the way and refusing simply to accept that this is the way things are and this is how they must be. They are living and speaking prophetically, because they believe that their own future depends on it. It is essential to believe that we can change things, that indeed we can change the world. This is what Christians have always believed. When Christians have acted upon this belief in obedience to Christ, extraordinary changes have taken place. From the growth of the early Christian church to the emancipation of slaves and the largely peaceful transition to democracy in South Africa, we can see and know that change is possible and that truth and justice are worth fighting for and, if necessary, dying for.

To follow Christ is to believe that his way is the way of hope and healing for all humankind and for all creation. The contemplative struggle is the way in which we live out this great conviction. This is how we will become part of the new thing which the Lord will do, in our own time, for the salvation and the healing of the nations and our sick and suffering earth.

9

Fire and rain

We are living in a time of unfolding environmental catastrophe. After decades of complacency and unheeded warnings, we are now face to face with fire and rain, with burning forests and homes and rising waters. These are the days of the climate emergency.

I know about fire and rain. Our world is a fragile system where nature can quickly turn from being our friend and mother to being our enemy and a terrifying foe. On the farm in South Africa where I grew up, we were well aware of how dependent we were on forces of nature beyond our control. There were long, hard months when no rain would fall and the crops would fail and the veld would be parched and dry. We would have to buy feed for the cattle, with money borrowed from the bank to which we were already heavily in debt. And then the dry Berg winds would blow, and my father would be constantly on the alert for any signs of smoke or fire on the horizon. When the sun beat down on the farm day after day, and the clouds came and went with no rain, fire became the great fear in all our minds.

One year, when I was 19, a fire started on a neighbour's farm. The winds picked up during the night and the fire started to spread. It jumped across into the pine forest on the sides of Majuba mountain, and then it became unstoppable. I still vividly remember driving the farm truck all day, from early in the morning, taking water to those who were trying to put out the flames as they spread and took hold. Our farmhouse had a thatched roof and we were in real danger of losing our home. My mother took all our most important documents and photographs and buried them in the vegetable garden. At one point I stopped for a few minutes and knelt down and cried out to God to save our home. The fire moved through the forest and took the house that my grandparents had built a few hundred yards away. Our house was spared. But my memory was seared forever by what happened that day.

This experience is now being spread, as by fire, across the globe. From Australia to the Amazon, from California to Borneo and Sumatra, we see that our home, our planet, is burning. The smoke rises in vast, dense clouds and obscures the sun, and even more carbon rises into the atmosphere. It gets worse and worse, and there is nothing we can do. We can fight the fires, but as I know, this kind of fire is too big, too terrifying, too powerful. We are at their mercy, and there is little mercy to be found when you are facing a fire that is out of control.

Then there is the rain, and the floods that the rain can bring. I always used to think of rain as something good, life-giving and benevolent. On the farm we longed for good rains. The rains brought renewal and life to the earth; the grass turned from brown to green and even the birds seemed to rejoice when the rains came. But in September 1987, I experienced another side to rain and rising water. I was a parish priest in Hilton, in KwaZulu-Natal, and one weekend I was attending a conference in nearby Pietermaritzburg. It started raining heavily on the Friday, and it continued all day Saturday and Sunday. On Monday the rain was still coming down hard. Flood warnings were being issued, and already there was widespread damage. Accurate information about the state of roads and bridges was increasingly hard to obtain. Towards the end of the 8.00 pm television news, the announcers said that they were receiving reports that the giant John Ross bridge over the Tugela river, linking Durban and Zululand, was gone. The bridge, along with a number of vehicles that were crossing it, had been washed out to sea by the power of the water. It continued to rain all day Monday, and I still recall the sound of the rain pounding down on the roof, no longer welcome and life-giving, but threatening, unstoppable and dreadful.

On Tuesday morning the rain finally stopped. We had lived through South Africa's worst natural disaster, which brought destruction and death on a vast scale. Around 25 inches of rain had fallen in our area in less than five days. In KwaZulu-Natal, nearly 400 people died in the floods and about 50,000 were left homeless. All over the region roads and houses and even factories had been washed away or ruined. A massive relief operation began to get underway. Many churches, including our own in Hilton, became centres for the collection and distribution of food, clothing, blankets, mattresses and other much-needed items, as well as money. The normal weekly activities of our church, the Church of the Ascension, came to a standstill as donations and gifts for flood relief poured in. We already had a well-established ministry network in the neighbouring area of Sweetwaters, where there was huge flood damage and desperate need. Virtually the whole church was mobilised for the task of sorting and distributing the gifts and donations to those who were most in need.

That flood seemed in 1987 to be a 'once in a hundred years' event. But now it seems like it was just a taste of things to come. Climate change is bringing torrential rains that cause unprecedented flooding in many parts of the world. As the ice melts in the Arctic, in Greenland and in Antarctica, global sea levels are widely predicted to rise by a metre or more by 2100.

The good earth weeps

Everywhere we look, we can see that we have failed to care for the world which God has made. One of the most telling phrases in the creation narrative, repeated several times, is this: 'And God saw that it was good' (Genesis 1:10–25). Genesis tells us of the unfolding creation of all things by God, the giver of life. At each key moment in the process of creation God seems to stop and survey all that he has made, and it is good in his eyes. We live in a wonderful world, but it has always been a world where there is tooth and claw, drought and flood, volcano and earthquake. Some of this, and the havoc that is wreaked, we do not understand. There are mysteries woven into the very fabric of God's creation and its great majesty and beauty. But at the heart of it all, the Bible tells us, is the goodness of the God who is the origin of all things, whose name is Love.

What we do know, however, is that sin, greed and selfishness lead to the spoiling and desecration of God's good purposes. What God has made to be good, rich and beautiful has become tarnished, broken and depleted. In May 2019 my wife and I were in KwaZulu-Natal visiting family and friends. We took a few days' break to stay in a small guesthouse on the coast, north of Durban. When I was a boy, my family often went to the Natal coast for holidays. We stayed in old cottages in small settlements that had sprung up along the Indian Ocean coast, such as Umhlali, Umdloti and Clansthal. So I jumped at the chance to go back to Umdloti for a few days, just to wander the beach and the rock pools and to swim in the Indian Ocean.

But it wasn't like it used to be. Where there was once coastal bush teeming with sunbirds and wild flowers, now there were rows and rows of holiday apartments. I used to pick up seashells scattered in profusion on the shore. Now there were hardly any seashells worth picking up; everywhere there was plastic waste and debris and rubbish. I used to watch my father fishing in the sea, and we would have freshly caught fish for supper, straight from the ocean. There were two or three men fishing, but they weren't catching anything. I am a keen birdwatcher, so I was looking for gulls and seabirds, but there weren't any of those either. I asked a local man why there were no seagulls. He replied, 'There's no fish, so there's no seagulls.'

The month of May in South Africa is usually a pleasantly cool time as midwinter approaches. But this year it was unbearably hot and humid, so I didn't spend much time on the beach at all; it was too hot. I did, however, come away having seen for myself what has happened to the beautiful coast of my childhood. It no longer exists, not as it used to be. It has been spoiled.

A contemplative heart is one that is aligned with the heart of God. As the love of God comes to rule our hearts, we find ourselves looking at others as God looks at them. We see with the eyes of love, of compassion, of mercy and of sorrow. We look at the world – at creation and at those around us – with the eyes of Jesus.

To look at the state of the world as it is today is to see a world that is in desperate need of healing and salvation. In so many ways it is a broken world, a world that has been spoiled. We are rushing headlong into the unravelling of the essential life-giving and life-sustaining balance of the natural world. The potential for untold suffering of both humans and other creatures is staring us in the face. The God of love calls us to turn from our foolish and self-centred ways and to return to his saving grace and goodness. When we place God at the centre, we find again our true humanity, our true selves, in Jesus and in his holy ways.

All of us share to some degree in the responsibility for what we have done to our planet. We all must come before God in sorrow and penitence over this. We know that the Lord hears the cries of his faithful and suffering children. We are told again and again, in the Psalms especially, that our God is a God who is merciful. He is slow to anger, and quick to forgive:

> The Lord is merciful and gracious,
>> slow to anger and abounding in steadfast love.
> He will not always accuse,
>> nor will he keep his anger forever.
> He does not deal with us according to our sins,
>> nor repay us according to our iniquities.
> For as the heavens are high above the earth,
>> so great is his steadfast love towards those who fear him;
> as far as the east is from the west,
>> so far he removes our transgressions from us.
> As a father has compassion for his children,
>> so the Lord has compassion for those who fear him.
> For he knows how we were made;
>> he remembers that we are dust.
> PSALM 103:8–14

So we cry to the Lord to have mercy on us and upon our broken world and our damaged and bleeding ecosystems. We do not give in to despair, even though the outlook at times is bleak. We are the people of hope, because we know that the all-powerful God of mercy hears our cries.

But having cried to the Lord for forgiveness and mercy, we must then live as those who care as God cares. A contemplative heart is a heart that loves as God loves. If our hearts are aligned with the heart of God, we must act. It is now a case of do or die. If we truly believe in the living God, we will live and act according to his will for our world. This is bound to involve a recognition that the ideology of consumerist capitalism is central to the crisis we face. For years the world of business has tended to see nature primarily as a resource to be exploited for human gain and profit. Dominion of nature for our own use and benefit seems to be written into the way things are in our present culture. To break free of this and still live within western society is almost impossible.

As a young white South African living in apartheid society, I and many others were asking: how do I live in this racist and oppressive society and yet maintain integrity and compassion, as a disciple of Jesus Christ? There are many similarities between the dilemma before us then and the challenges we now face. We might be okay, but the world is in a bad way and time is running out. These are times which call for radical and prophetic action. Young leaders and activists, such as Greta Thunberg, are showing the way. We need a radical non-acceptance of all that is not true and just and holy. The greatest example of such a way of life is to be found in the life and teaching of Jesus. As Christians we believe in the one who is Christ in us, the hope of glory. We now have to work out what this means in terms of how we live for Christ in our daily lives.

Our culture is at war with nature. If Christ is in us, we will face a constant struggle in trying to avoid being compromised by an ideology whose purpose is to serve and gratify the desires of the false self.

Instead we work to bring an end to the war and to bring hope to those around us. Jesus says, 'Blessed are the peacemakers, for they will be called children of God' (Matthew 5:9). In order to be peacemakers, we first have to be those who speak and act upon the truth. It is no good simply saying 'Peace, peace', when there is no peace. We speak the truth to our culture, and we seek day by day to act and live with authenticity and compassion. We offer our lives, as Jesus did upon the cross, in order that we may share in the ministry of reconciliation:

> All this is from God, who reconciled us to himself through Christ, and has given us the ministry of reconciliation; that is, in Christ God was reconciling the world to himself, not counting their trespasses against them, and entrusting the message of reconciliation to us.
> 2 CORINTHIANS 5:18–19

Then we leave the future in God's hands, because we have done what we can and must do. The rest, and the future, we leave to him.

Pollution: what you can do

In June 1971, when I was editor of *NUX*, we published a main feature on environmental pollution and the dangers of unchecked industrial and urban development. The article was titled 'Where are we going?' and showed large photographs of the vast sprawl of the city of Los Angeles in 1971 'looming out of the smog of its own making'.[38] The article was intended to make people sit up and take notice of the dangers of failing to care properly for the environment. We included, on another page, a section entitled 'Pollution: what you can do'. This is what we said:

Cutting waste
- Don't buy products that are packed in containers of plastic, metal or wax, that don't break down in water or the natural environment.

- Always select products wrapped in minimum packaging.
- Buy milk in returnable glass bottles (and return them).
- Use cloth instead of paper for towelling, napkins and handkerchiefs.
- Always keep and use a litter bag in your car.

Cleaning and saving water
- Take briefer showers, and don't overwater your garden.
- Don't use pesticides, herbicides and insecticides, especially DDT. Rather use a fly swatter and pull out weeds by hand.
- Buy no colour-dyed tissue paper.
- Convert to organic gardening – make compost from your garbage, leaves and grass cuttings.

Cleaning air
- Don't use your car if you can walk, ride a bicycle or take a bus.
- If you need a car, buy a small one and get an anti-pollution device fitted.
- Use fuels for fireplaces sparingly.

Miscellaneous
- Don't buy animal fur or leather.
- Don't have more than two children.
- Don't eat highly processed foods.
- Exchange your motor mower for a manual one.
- Eliminate unnecessary electrical appliances.
- Generating electricity heavily pollutes both air and water.[39]

I was 20 years old when we published this article. Now, almost 50 years later, I read this and I wonder, over all the years that have passed since then, how we can have been so blind. For the past 50 years I have aimed to live by these guidelines, and by others, in order to care for this beautiful world which we have been given. Some things have changed, but most of what we wrote then is still relevant. Many things, however, are now a lot worse, and the challenges which confront us are far greater than they were 50 years ago. It is not difficult for anyone to see the mainly small, practical ways in which we can and should act in our daily lives to care for our environment. All of us can make a difference, and, certainly for myself, these guidelines are still a good place to start.

At a deeper level, my heart is increasingly drawn to see our world as God sees it, with the eyes of his unfailing compassion, goodness and mercy. Ultimately, we look to God our creator to save us and help us. We cannot do this on our own. Our flesh, our sinful, self-centred human nature, is weak, and we turn so easily to our own ways. The climate emergency is a call to all humankind to return to those things which lead to peace and to community and to the flourishing of all life on earth.

10

Black consciousness and human liberation

Central to the Christian gospel is the understanding that every human being is loved by God and is precious in his eyes. We are all equally valuable and significant. Our race and our cultural background are part of who we are; they are part of the way God has made us. This is who I am, and I am loved by God, infinitely and unconditionally. There are no hierarchies in the kingdom of God. The apostle Paul says, 'There is no longer Jew or Greek, there is no longer slave or free, there is no longer male and female; for all of you are one in Christ Jesus' (Galatians 3:28).

Every person, no matter who they are or where they come from, is a wonderful, sacred being – a human being, able to love and be loved, to create, to feel and think and to suffer. We are all 'fearfully and wonderfully made' (Psalm 139:14). I dare not ever think that I am somehow better because of my race or nationality.

Black consciousness, as articulated by Steve Biko and his colleagues, understood this well. They were concerned with the full restoration of dignity and worth to black people. Their particular context was apartheid, but the philosophy of black consciousness is relevant wherever racism is a problem. Black consciousness, according to Steve Biko, 'makes the black man see himself as a being, entire in himself, and not as an extension of a broom or additional leverage to some machine.'[40] Black consciousness is about personhood; it is saying that people matter because of who they are in themselves. Human beings are not mere units of production whose chief purpose is to keep the economy growing or to produce profits. For Biko there was no question that apartheid was originally introduced in South African politics for economic reasons.[41]

Black consciousness, according to Biko, is directly linked to the quest for a true humanity and is not just another form of racism:

> Some will charge that we are racist, but these people are using exactly the values we reject. We do not have the power to subjugate anyone. We are merely responding to provocation in the most realistic possible way. Racism does not only imply exclusion of one race by another – it always presupposes that the exclusion is for the purposes of subjugation. Blacks have had enough experience as objects of racism not to wish to turn the tables.[42]

For Biko black consciousness was ultimately part of a much greater vision:

> We have set out on a quest for true humanity, and somewhere on the distant horizon we can see the glittering prize. Let us march forth with courage and determination, drawing strength from our common plight and our brotherhood. In time we shall be in a position to bestow upon South Africa the greatest gift possible – a more human face.[43]

Through UCM and other student organisations, I began to see the potential for a very different South African society from the one in which I had grown up, a South Africa with a more human face. I met and listened to young black leaders who had so much to offer. But I knew also that they were speaking from the daily experience of white supremacy, police violence and institutionalised oppression. I listened to the anger of black students, and I knew that some were increasingly hostile to any idea of working together with whites.

This presented serious challenges to young white people who saw themselves as Christian. It quickly became clear to us that for many black people, Christianity was the religion of the oppressor. When you have a government that premeditatedly plans to destroy people, how can you call that government Christian? I knew that I had to learn to recognise evil when it was laid bare before my eyes. Then I had to oppose it with all my might. The system was causing appalling suffering to black people, and I came to believe that our task as Christians was to work to collapse the system and to replace it with a just, free and non-racial society based as much as possible on the teachings of Jesus.

Steve Biko has much to teach us in the enormous challenges of our own time. His boldness, his compassion and humanity and his unwillingness to play games with a system that was fundamentally unjust and dehumanising: all of these speak to us about what following Christ might mean for us now.

Black consciousness was never primarily a political movement, and it was never closed to dialogue and friendship with white activists. Ian M. Macqueen says:

> No doubt, Black Consciousness bore the personal imprint of its key intellectual and political leader and there were those less disposed to such open engagement, but the strength of the Black Consciousness message during its historical moment was also the result of its ability to *convert* and because its message resonated with the utopian hopes of radical Christians and socialists. A call to maturity, personal growth and a qualified openness was inherent in the political vision of the leaders of Black Consciousness, for whom the ideas were more of 'a way of being' than a political orthodoxy, and in which personal liberation necessarily preceded political freedom.[44]

Aelred Stubbs was an Anglican priest and member of the Community of the Resurrection who worked in South Africa from 1960 until 1977. He was principal of St Peter's Theological College when it moved to Alice, in the Eastern Cape, and became a component part of the ecumenical Federal Theological Seminary. It was here that Father Stubbs first came into contact with the Biko family. He became a close friend of Biko and a number of other leading black political activists. He visited them in detention and provided spiritual guidance and support to many who had been banned or banished. Undergirding everything was his practice of contemplative prayer.

In 1977 Father Stubbs returned to the UK for the funeral of his mother. The South African government then withdrew his permission to return to South Africa. He returned instead to an Anglican contemplative community in a remote corner of Lesotho, to the Masite Mission of the Society of the Precious Blood. There he started writing a letter to friends, reflecting on his experiences in his ministry over the previous 17 years in South Africa. While he was writing this letter, Father Stubbs received news of Biko's death in detention on 12 September 1977. Macqueen writes:

> His letter stopped abruptly and, inserting the date, 14 September 1977, he attempted to articulate his feelings. 'Nearly twenty-four hours after receiving the news I am unable to grasp its full horror', he began. He had been requested by the Archbishop of Cape Town and church leaders in South Africa and Britain to remain silent for fear that public comment may jeopardise his visa arrangement. However, Stubbs could not remain silent. 'Steve Biko was the finest human being I have known', he wrote. 'He has been to me a son, a leader, and a friend. He is my brother in Christ. He had proved himself fit to take his place with Nelson Mandela and Robert Sobukwe as the true leaders, not of the blacks only, but of all the people of South Africa.'[45]

On 25 September 1977 Stubbs preached a sermon in the chapel at the Masite mission at a service commemorating Biko's life and passing. Speaking of black consciousness, 'Stubbs recognised it as "an astonishing achievement, this restoration to a people of its humanity. And not only to blacks, because it is whites who are dehumanised by the ideology of racial superiority even more than blacks."'[46]

This, of course, is not to say that whites suffered more than blacks because of apartheid. That would be absurd. But Stubbs and Biko understood that racism dehumanises both the oppressor and the oppressed, and both need liberation.

Liberation is all about setting the captives free. Racism oppresses and dehumanises. In South Africa and in many other countries, racism has caused immense suffering to black people in particular. Black consciousness sought to convert both the oppressed and the oppressor. The message and gospel of Jesus Christ has the same purpose, and I came to see that in South Africa both messages were essential. We needed political change and liberation, but, much more than this, we needed a change of hearts. Each of us needed to discover that we and all our fellow South Africans were created by God in his image, and all were loved by God, equally and infinitely.

God's purpose for all humankind is that we should be one in Christ Jesus. Jesus has broken down the hostility and the barriers that divide us, once and for all (Ephesians 2:14). His great prayer in John 17 is that we should all be one, just as he and the Father are one. The purpose of the Christian life is that we should be like Jesus and find our true humanity in him. The relationship of union between Jesus and the Father is the model of what it means to live a life of Christlike love and to discover our true humanity in the image of God. In the richness of our diversity we learn to live together in unity and harmony.

Jesus prays:

> As you, Father, are in me and I am in you, may they also be in us, so that the world may believe that you have sent me. The glory that you have given me I have given them, so that they may be one, as we are one, I in them and you in me, that they may become completely one, so that the world may know that you have sent me and have loved them even as you have loved me.
> JOHN 17:21–23

The glory which the Father gave to Jesus, Jesus has given to us for this purpose: that we may be united in a common shared humanity. And, says Jesus, this is for another, greater purpose: that the world may know that the Father sent Jesus and has loved each one of us as he loved Jesus, his own Son.

11

Tackling poverty and injustice

I was walking down a street in Nelspruit having just arrived the previous day on a flight from London via Johannesburg. Nelspruit, or Mbombela as it is now known, is a large town in the Mpumalanga province of South Africa, close to the Kruger National Park game reserve. In some ways it is a thriving town, with an airport, a large hospital and the impressive Mbombela Stadium, which was built for the 2010 football World Cup. But everywhere I looked, as I walked along, I saw poverty and need. Men stood by the side of the road, waiting for taxis or just standing around watching the traffic go by. The Mpumalanga province has one of the highest rates of unemployment in South Africa. In 2019 South Africa's unemployment rate stood at 27.6%, while for Mpumalanga it was 34.2%.[47]

Women walked past me, some carrying white or blue plastic carrier bags, faces etched with the weight of a life of caring for others on very limited means. The average domestic worker in South Africa usually supports four people, including themselves, on an income of between R2001 (£90) and R3000 (£135) a month, with no additional support from government grants. 71% of domestic workers are single mothers who are the main breadwinner of their household.[48]

I was born not far from here, in a coal-mining town called Witbank (now known as Emalahleni, meaning the 'place of coal'), which is also in the Mpumalanga province. I know this part of the world; in many ways it is part of me, part of who I am. Every time I return here I am brought back to some fundamental realities about our life on this planet, our so-called 'global village'. Again and again I have to face the reality of the dysfunctional, unjust and unequal world that we have made for ourselves. I live in the affluent 'first world', the developed world. I benefit at every turn because of this. From healthcare to pensions, from access to cheap food to the ability to travel widely, I know that I am incredibly privileged. I am thankful for what I have, but I am also deeply unsettled and uncomfortable about it. I have so much, and so many people have so little.

My own convictions about poverty and inequality were formed in my student days. As we became more aware of the political and social realities of life in South Africa, the only possible response for us was to do something about it. It's no good just thinking about it, feeling bad and vaguely hoping that the problem will go away. In South Africa at that time, taking action against poverty and injustice inevitably meant conflict and confrontation. Looking back, the situation seemed so urgent and important that we did not hesitate. We committed ourselves wholeheartedly to work for change. We knew that our own futures, and the future of our country and our world, depended on it.

The Wages Commission

When I was a member of the Students' Representative Council (SRC) in 1970–71, we set up what was called the Wages Commission. This was initially a subcommittee of the SRC, set up to investigate the wages paid by the University of Natal to its own black staff. Within a few months the role of the Wages Commission had expanded significantly. The work of the commission was led by a student friend, Mike Murphy, who was head of the National Catholic Federation of Students' (NCFS) Justice and Peace Commission. In addition to pressing the university to pay all its employees a living wage regardless of race, the commission began to raise awareness of wage disparities in the wider local economy. We realised that many local employers were paying their employees wages far below the poverty datum line, the minimum income required to provide the basic essentials of life.

We also realised that there were channels available to us to address this situation. We discovered that the Industrial Wages Board met regularly to examine and reassess the wage scales in various industries. The board had the power to raise the minimum wage levels, but unless spokesmen or women for the workers attended the board meetings to explain and show in hard figures that they were not able to live adequately on the present salaries, nothing would be done. It was clear that this offered a tremendous opportunity for student members of the Wages Commission, over and above campus activity. The Wages Commission began to find out when and where these Industrial Wages Board meetings were due to take place, and then make sure that workers knew about them. This involved contacting individual workers and also distributing pamphlets at factories and places of employment.

The impact of the work of the Wages Commission increased rapidly, and the government soon became alarmed. In November 1976, Mike Murphy and Pat Horn and a number of other student activists who were involved in the Wages Commission were given five-year banning orders. This meant that they were prohibited from attending meetings of any kind, speaking in public or publishing or distributing any written material. The banned person was not permitted ever to be with more than one other person at a time. The penalty for breaking the rules of a banning order was up to five years in prison. Apart from anything else, this meant that they could no longer continue their university studies.

In 1971 there was a new sense of urgency among many white South African students about the situation we found ourselves in. We were looking for ways to contribute to and bring about change. In October of that year, I wrote in an editorial in *NUX*:

> The need for reform is something which is becoming increasingly plain as we examine virtually every facet of our society and our university – certainly there is enough to give every socially aware person on this campus something to involve himself [*sic*] in and to work for. It is encouraging to see that more and more students seem to be realising this, and the recent pamphlet distribution

campaigns, the response to SAVS project at Pomeroy and the phenomenal success of Envirac all bear this out.[49]

In the editorial I was also highly critical of the apathetic white students who failed to make their contribution. Many students preferred to just get on with their own lives, have a good time and hopefully leave university with a degree. I wrote, 'They simply cannot be bothered, and it is this idleness and apathy in the face of such opportunities for learning, acting and helping as being a student offers that truly condemns them, especially when these opportunities are open to so few in our society.'[50]

It seems to me that this speaks directly to the situation in which our world now finds itself. All of us are caught up in a world of increasingly urgent crises and challenges. We know that we cannot simply carry on as before. Are we ready to make our contribution and to work for change, for a different, a better and more just, world? Or are we simply hoping that our own position will not be affected, and that we can leave others to do the work of bringing about change?

In addressing the issues of poverty and wage inequality there are a number of ways in which we can make our contribution. The work of the Wages Commission took people like Mike Murphy to the front line of confronting entrenched business and political interests. It takes courage to do this. This is the work of advocacy, of speaking out for the exploited among us. It often leads to conflict, and it can be very costly. It certainly was for Mike Murphy, Pat Horn and many others, white and black.

One of the most serious problems for the church in the affluent developed countries of the west is the tendency to concentrate on the personal dimensions of sin. Many Christians in these countries remain largely blind to the institutional and structural dimensions of sin. When the ways of the 'me-first' false self are in control, then we are living lives of sin. This applies not only to our individual lives but to communities and to nations. It is vital that the church recognises that our society and culture are riddled with dubious and sinful assumptions about how we should live. We exploit the planet. We exploit our neighbour. We ignore the cries of the hungry, the destitute and the refugee. We store up goods for ourselves and treat God as an accomplice in our plans and schemes. For all this we need repentance, just as much as we need repentance from personal sin.

Another way in which we as students were able to help the poor and contribute to change was through the SAVS projects. SAVS was a student voluntary service organisation at Natal University, led by Charlie Manicom, a close friend of mine. Charlie and I both lived in the Malherbe Residence in 1971, and we were both raided by Security Police on the morning of Sunday 24 October. Charlie was the son of a Methodist minister and was deeply committed to helping others and working to make a difference for good in society. In July 1971, under Charlie's leadership, SAVS embarked on an ambitious new project, to build a clinic in the rural village of Pomeroy. Pomeroy is a remote community of mainly Zulu people, far from any major urban centre. When we started building, we worked alongside a small clinic run by Roman Catholic sisters, who, despite the wholly inadequate facilities, delivered over 600 babies there each year. This was an area of extreme poverty, with many suffering from malnutrition. Some four or five nurses were responsible for seeing and caring for up to 250 patients a day. People would walk for 20 or 30 miles or even more in order to be seen at the clinic. As Charlie wrote, 'One doesn't have to look far at Pomeroy for a reason to work.'[51]

Groups of students would go out to Pomeroy over weekends and vacations with sleeping bags and food. We slept in an empty house near the site and cooked our own food. We dug foundations, levelled the area and laid the concrete floor. I remember the sweat pouring off my back in the hot sun, as I revelled in doing some hard labour after weeks of study and books. In twelve months, the new clinic was complete. It had eleven rooms, to be used for the maternity cases dealt with at Pomeroy. Over 1,500 people attended the opening of the clinic in August 1972 by the Roman Catholic bishop of Ermelo. At the time it was one of the most ambitious student building schemes ever undertaken in South Africa.

There are many ways to tackle poverty and injustice. For myself, in South Africa at that time, it was imperative that everyone should be doing something to help others and bring about change. I could see no excuse for apathy and indifference. Jesus says, 'From everyone to whom much has been given, much will be required; and from the one to whom much has been entrusted, even more will be demanded' (Luke 12:48). As we look around at the state of the world right now, these words call each one of us to action. We all have gifts to offer; we can all make a contribution, no matter how small. As Greta Thunberg says in the title of her book, *No One Is Too Small to Make a Difference*.

In all of this we have before us the example of Jesus himself. He did not hesitate to challenge the hypocrisy of the Pharisees, the religious rulers and teachers. He overthrew the tables of the moneychangers in the temple and drove them out, saying, 'It is written, "My house shall be called a house of prayer", but you are making it a den of robbers' (Matthew 21:13). He fed the hungry, and he healed the sick. Wherever he encountered people who were suffering, he acted to bring relief and restoration. He declared that he had come to 'proclaim release to the captives and recovery of sight to the blind, to let the oppressed go free' (Luke 4:18). He said:

> I was hungry and you gave me food, I was thirsty and you gave me something to drink, I was a stranger and you welcomed me, I was naked and you gave me clothing, I was sick and you took care of me, I was in prison and you visited me… Truly I tell you, just as you did it to one of the least of these who are members of my family, you did it to me.
> MATTHEW 25:35–36, 40

The words and example of Jesus speak to us in our own time and situation, urgently and unambiguously. The question we face is this: how then should we live? Obeying Christ in a rapidly changing world is likely to be costly and demanding, but it is also the way to hope and healing and to making all things new. To be a Christian is to act in faith, to love one another as Christ has loved us and to trust always that 'in all these things we are more than conquerors through him who loved us' (Romans 8:37).

12

The cost of living

During the 1980s and early 1990s I worked as a parish priest in the Diocese of Natal. These were days of turmoil and violence, when we had no idea what the future might hold for South Africa. But on 27 April 1994, we experienced the miracle of our first democratic election, and the transfer of power to the ANC.[52] I voted in these elections on a day that I and millions of others will never forget. It was the culmination of years of struggle, of hoping and praying and working for a just and free South Africa. It is still hard to comprehend the extraordinary transformation that happened on that amazing day.

Soon after the elections, I came to England for a sabbatical study break at St John's College, Nottingham. During this time, I made enquiries about possible job opportunities in the United Kingdom. I was reluctant to leave South Africa, but my wife, Alison, is British and she was keen to return to the UK, in particular to resume her teaching career there.

Somewhat to my surprise, I was offered an appointment in a parish on the north side of Cambridge, adjoining the newly developed science park. We moved in August 1994, and I was immediately struck by the difference in expectations and standards of living between my new parishioners and those of my friends and colleagues in South Africa. While the whole of South Africa had been caught up in the long struggle to break free of apartheid, in the 1980s and early 1990s a huge economic change had taken place in Britain. The process continued apace through the 1990s and into the new century. Many people found themselves able to afford to buy and to do things that their parents could only have dreamed about.

We had never owned a computer at that point, but everyone I met seemed to have a computer in their home. Even their teenage children had their own computers. To me a computer was hugely expensive, way beyond what I could have afforded as an Anglican priest in South Africa. When I saw what people were spending on Christmas and birthday presents for their children and young people, I was astonished. This was more than many people I knew in South Africa would be earning in a month. I looked at the prices of shirts and trousers in a department store. I couldn't believe it; this was five times more than I would have ever paid in South Africa. But now I was earning pounds, not South African rand. Suddenly I was becoming a rich man. I had never had so much money in my life. I went out and bought a six-year-old SAAB car and drove away thinking, 'This is mine. How did this happen?'

The 1990s were a new era of prosperity for many people in Britain. The older generation was increasingly retiring on generous pensions. It was becoming normal for people from ordinary backgrounds to enjoy two or three overseas holidays a year. Cars that I always considered to be exclusive luxury models were becoming mainstream. Many families now owned two or even three cars. The pound sterling was becoming more and more valuable. Young people could leave school, work for six months in a local hotel or restaurant, and then travel around the world on the pounds they had earned. Never had there been so much opportunity to do whatever you wanted at a price you could afford.

But all of this has come at a significant cost. The cost has been paid by many people, both in Britain and in other parts of the world. The cost of this way of living for some fortunate ones has been paid by the 'left behinds' – the low-paid and the forgotten millions in the developing world. They are the ones who grow the coffee, the flowers and the fruit that others enjoy. They are the ones who make the clothes and the shoes, the phones and the gadgets. We live in a deeply unequal world. Income and wealth inequality is one of the distinguishing features of our age. These issues of poverty and inequality face every city and town and community across the developed world. Many of us live in comfort and affluence, but there are also many among us who are struggling each day to make ends meet. Even more stark is the vast inequality in the cost and standard of living between the rich, developed nations and the impoverished countries, particularly in Africa.

Len Abrams is a South African who has worked for many years for the World Bank in helping poor communities in Africa gain access to clean and sustainable water supplies. He is also an Anglican priest, now living in England. Len described how, around four years previously, he visited a rural village in southern Zimbabwe. They had been provided with access to a small dam, and they told Len how incredibly privileged they felt to have this dam, because they were now able to grow food and to sell some of what they produced. They were asked, 'How much income do you make from the sale of food?' So they huddled together and talked about it, and they said that per family per year, they made about US$120, which is about £80 per family per year. This is the equivalent in UK terms to one large supermarket trolley of food, and yet they were able to say that they felt incredibly privileged.

Len described to me how he then saw a group of three children standing nearby in a field. It was the middle of the week and they should have been in school. So Len asked them, 'Why are you not in school? What is your situation here?' They said their mother was working as a domestic worker for a family in Johannesburg. They didn't know where their father was. They lived with their grandparents, and they didn't have the $20 a term that they needed to pay their school fees. 'And as we were standing around in a group, we probably had enough spare cash in our pockets to pay the school fees for all three of them for a year,' said Len. 'There's another generation gone. The difference is so massive that I just don't see how Africa is ever going to pull out of it.'

Len speaks persuasively about the desperate need and poverty across much of sub-Saharan Africa. There is a view among advocates of globalisation that poverty is slowly but surely being rolled back across the developing world through free international trade. But the reality of ordinary life across much of Africa does not bear this out. I am writing this in the year of the Covid-19 pandemic, and Len, among many others, is involved in assessing the possible impact of Covid-19 in Africa. To create some form of comparison, Len looked at the HIV-AIDS situation in southern Africa. In 2018, 610,000 new cases of HIV-AIDS were recorded, and over 300,000 died as a consequence of the disease. Africans have a lot of experience of plagues and diseases that kill many thousands of people. This is yet another disparity which is often overlooked or forgotten. Most people in sub-Saharan Africa simply do not have ready access even to good primary healthcare, let alone complex high-tech modern surgery and treatments.

The more you dig into this, the more you realise that there is a vast chasm between these two worlds. Len says that he travels a lot between Africa and Europe as part of his work. People often ask him, 'Don't you get whacked with jet lag?' Len says, 'Jet lag is not a problem. The emotional problem of moving from one universe to another – that's what gets me.' I know what he means; I get this too.

The question that many of us face is this: if we know the reality of what is happening in our world right now, how then do we live? How can we live with integrity and hope, when we are aware of these levels of inequality and deprivation? For those of us who have spent many years living in Africa, these questions are very familiar. Many of us have struggled over many years to work out a way to live with the privileges of our race, education and upbringing. If I go out for a meal in a restaurant, I am usually aware in some part of my consciousness that the money we are spending on one meal could feed a family in Africa for weeks, if not months. I know this, and I can never forget it. I suspect this is healthy for me, because it is an ever-present check on my own capacity for self-indulgence and for giving in to the pleasures of retail therapy.

If we are willing to honestly face these issues of acting justly and living generously, then we have to be asking questions about the way we spend our money. In an affluent society this can be enormously complex. It is a matter of comparison, because we can all look at those who have more than we do, as well as those who have less. Some live in very large houses with extensive gardens, and there is nothing that is necessarily wrong with this. In order to live with integrity, however, each of us must examine our own hearts and motives. What are we really living for? How willing are we to share what we have and to give what we have to others who are in desperate need? We have to ask ourselves some searching questions, both in the light of global inequalities and also in the light of the teaching of Jesus Christ. Unless we are willing to do this, we cannot credibly claim to be disciples or followers of Jesus. Jesus says, 'Not everyone who says to me, "Lord, Lord," will enter the kingdom of heaven, but only one who does the will of my Father in heaven' (Matthew 7:21).

Fresh Hope

A good place to begin to work out a Christ-centred response to income and wealth inequality is in one's own local area or community. My wife and I are members of St George's Church in Stamford, Lincolnshire. This is a large, well-attended church in the centre of an attractive, thriving town. But, as many of us who live here know, this town has a significant problem with poverty and deprivation. Over the past eight years or so, St George's has developed a major focus of work, which is called Fresh Hope. This is an umbrella project for a wide range of services provided by or through St George's for disadvantaged families and individuals. We also work together with other local churches and with charities such as Christians against Poverty (CAP), Stamford Foodbank and Stamford Household Essentials Project (SHEP), which provides furniture to those moving into empty council properties.

Every day desperate people arrive at the St George's Church office, the Hub, looking for help. They know that here they will find people who will accept them and listen to them, no matter what the problem is. It could be that they are homeless and rough sleeping or struggling for food or fuel. They may have housing issues or be struggling with mental health problems. Many of them simply don't know where else to turn.

Louise Rose is our Fresh Hope community projects manager, and she also manages Hope House, a house in Stamford for two tenants who would otherwise be homeless. Louise says:

> When people come to us they are met with love. Non-judge-mental, non-superficial love. That may look like a cup of tea and a listening ear or a tent and a bag of shopping. We try to meet the immediate practical need first and then work with the individual to address the reason for the need. And we recognise that most people who end up so desperate that they come to us have a host of issues from the past as well as the present. We can help them untangle their issues if we can begin a relation-ship with them that is long-term. It's not necessarily that people have made bad choices, but that they've had to deal with bad things happening to them which would fell the most competent of people.[53]

One example of this is the story of Maggie (not her real name), who used to ask for food bank vouchers every week and was constantly coming to the Hub requesting money for various things. Experience has taught us to give out money only rarely, because that is only ever a short-term solution, which some people abuse. It is better to support and help people to find their own way out of their problems. Louise says:

> We worked out that the main reason Maggie came was because she was lonely, so we invited her to Connect [our community cafe]. Slowly Maggie has moved from sitting near the door at Connect, to taking part in the banquet of cake given by our volunteers and to immersing herself in the community around the craft table. Recently she was encouraged to have a go at knitting and was given some wool to take home. After Christmas, Maggie brought me a small purse she had knitted herself. She

is so proud of what she achieved: pride in herself seemed an emotion foreign to her. She is also asking for far fewer food bank vouchers now.

One day Maggie brought us a letter to read because she is illiterate. The letter was an eviction notice due to rent arrears. We referred Maggie through to P3 (a charity supporting people with housing issues). We discovered that the reason why Maggie hadn't been paying her rent was because she had not fully grasped what needed to be paid and how. Maggie was referred through to CAP for her debt and to CAP Life Skills to help her to gain the skills to move forward with more understanding. In the end Maggie had to leave her property and the SHEP crew were called on to help move Maggie and her possessions to a family member's house.

There are no neat endings to this story. Maggie is still living in poverty and is yet to find a home to call her own. She still struggles to budget, but she is trying! Life is still challenging for her because her schooling was such that she never learned to read. Like many of our clients, their problems started in child-hood. But she has come a long way over the last year. She holds her head higher, she is closer to being debt free, she is achieving things for herself. She is part of a community and feels accepted. She has been prayed with on many occasions. Our hope and prayer is that one day she will come to know Jesus, but mean-while she is absorbing his love through the love of his people.[54]

Throughout the gospel we see Jesus seeking out the outcasts and the 'left behinds' in their communities. Jesus reaches out to those whom society has turned their back on – the judged, the forgotten, the trampled on. Jesus stands up for these people. He speaks love and worth to them, and he gives them value; from Zacchaeus the tax collector to the woman caught in adultery, Jesus brings hope and restoration to the outcasts, and he asks us to do the same. Jesus says, 'But when you give a banquet, invite the poor, the crippled, the lame and the blind. And you will be blessed' (Luke 14:13–14).

Rebecca Winfrey works alongside Louise in Fresh Hope and supports members of the community and congregation who are in need. Rebecca says:

> It's challenging work. We frequently have to live with unsolved problems. We turn to prayer a lot because we have frequently reached the end of what we can do. The people we care about experience frequent setbacks and some make unwise choices, but they keep coming. Every week at Friday Connect we marvel that about 70 people keep coming, and we can only conclude that the love of Jesus is what draws them. We are privileged to keep working with Him to transform lives.[55]

Our goal in Fresh Hope is not simply to do things for people who are in need, but also to build relationships which are rooted and grounded in the love of Jesus. This is the local church in action, serving the poor in the love of Jesus. If we are to follow the example and teaching of Jesus, this is what it's all about. The letter of James says:

> What good is it, my brothers and sisters, if you say you have faith but do not have works? Can faith save you? If a brother or sister is naked and lacks daily food, and one of you says to them, 'Go in peace; keep warm and eat your fill', and yet you do not supply their bodily needs, what is the good of that? So faith by itself, if it has no works, is dead.
> JAMES 2:14–17

How shall we then live?

To follow Jesus at this time in history means that we cannot be indifferent or apathetic about poverty and inequality. We all need to act in some way or other. If we do not act, then, apart from anything else, our faith will have little or no credibility for millions who look to the church for an example. Many young people are appalled by the inequalities of wealth and opportunity that they see around them.

They long for a society and a world which is fairer to all, a world which is more just and more equal. So the question again, for all who call ourselves Christian, is this: how then shall we live?

It is important to recognise the complexity of working out a Christian response to these issues. We are faced with not only personal choices about how we spend our money, but also structural injustice and an economic system that corrupts many of those who benefit from it. Wealth is more than just a commodity. Wealth has the power to get under our skin and infect us with a curious blindness, a sickness of the heart. The affluent society has impoverished us by making us wealthy. Jesus calls our attention to this in stark terms:

> Then Jesus said to his disciples, 'Truly I tell you, it will be hard for a rich person to enter the kingdom of heaven. Again I tell you, it is easier for a camel to go through the eye of a needle than for someone who is rich to enter the kingdom of God.' When the disciples heard this, they were greatly astounded and said, 'Then who can be saved?' But Jesus looked at them and said, 'For mortals it is impossible, but for God all things are possible.'
> MATTHEW 19:23–26

When I was a parish priest in South Africa, I wrote a book about our own local church's response to the needs of those in desperate poverty within our area. Reflecting on the challenge of living alongside people who had so little, I wrote:

> We need to be 'normal' and yet different, those who are able to enjoy life, to go out for a meal occasionally, to listen to music and watch sporting events, but not those who are totally caught up in these things without being mindful of the needs and suffering of others. This is not an easy balance to find. For us, the community of the local church is a great help in working towards this balance. Some in the church are intensely concerned with the poor and the demands of the gospel. They need to be helped not to take themselves too seriously, to relax and yield their

concerns to God. Others are easily caught up in the concerns and pleasures of the world, and they need the prophetic challenge of others to help them to be faithful disciples of the Lord Jesus.[56]

Each of us has to work out our own response to the economic realities of our society and the needs that surround us. To follow Jesus means living simply, entering into relationships with the poor, giving generously, caring for the environment and breaking with consumerism once and for all. Faith without works is dead.

13

War and peace

When I was 17, some four weeks after leaving high school, I began military training in the South African army. Military service was compulsory for all young white South African males. At that point in my life I did not question this; it was just what we did. We were all required by law to do some form of military service. My first experience of adult life after leaving boarding school was life in the army. It was an experience that I will never forget.

I was sent to the Danie Theron Combat School near Kimberley in the Northern Cape province. Kimberley is famous for diamond mining and for the 'big hole', a vast hole in the ground, excavated by miners in the 19th century. But I saw almost nothing of Kimberley. We all arrived by train in the first week of January, in the height of summer. When we arrived, we were given military haircuts and issued with rifles, bayonets, uniforms, boots and overalls. Civilian life was a thing of the past. We had to learn that we were units in a military machine and that we would obey every command without question. Under no circumstances were we ever to think for ourselves.

We were woken each morning at 4.00 am to get ready for inspection. Breakfast was at 6, and then at 7.00 am we were on the parade ground. The whole morning was spent being drilled in the blazing sun. The afternoons were for bush craft, shooting and combat training. The evenings were spent getting ready for the next morning's inspection. Lights out was at 10.45 pm.

I found the experience of being in the army utterly dehumanising. The brutality, the endless swearing, the loss of all normal human dignity – being systematically reduced to the lowest common denominator of human experience and behaviour. Survival was all that mattered, just getting through another day. All the niceties of civilised behaviour went out the window. It was intended to be tough, and it was. There is no place for weakness in the army and in a war situation. It is survival of the fittest. I soon learnt that the best approach to army life was to keep my head down, do what I was told and never volunteer for anything. Just get through this and get out the other side. If they didn't crush me, I would still have a life when this was over.

I remember lying on the rifle range while a sadistic corporal walked up and down lashing with a belt the legs and backs of anyone who was not lying in exactly the correct position for shooting. I remember the bayonet training when we were told to give a loud scream as we plunged the bayonet into the enemy. I remember doing leopard crawl on my stomach through the thorn veld in the afternoon sun, and learning to implement curfews and road blocks and to deal with unlawful assemblies. I still have my notes on this:

> Provision for escape of mob must be made. Specific target will be given to a specific marksman. Front rank is to face the crowd. Should the firing of a single shot not have the desired effect this may be repeated as desired. After firing, cease fire, empty rifles, pick up doppies [empty cartridge shells] and hand over to police. Clear the area, restore law and order as fast as possible. Use conventional principles of warfare.

This was nine years after the Sharpeville massacre of 1960, when the South African police had opened fire on a crowd of demonstrators in a township, killing 69 people and injuring another 180. On 16 June 1976 in Soweto, police opened fire on a crowd of schoolchildren who were demonstrating against Afrikaans as the language of instruction in black schools. It is estimated that up to 700 people died in the Soweto uprising. These were the kinds of situations that we were being trained to deal with.

After my basic training I was able to go to university, but for some years I was regularly called up for training camps and guard duty. We were required to guard key strategic sites in the Durban area, such as the oil refinery, the airport and the harbour. After five years I received a letter asking me to return all my army kit and my rifle, as I was no longer required for regular military call-ups. I suspect that by this point student activists like myself were not regarded as being suitable people for the work of the South African Defence Force. It was with an overwhelming sense of relief that I handed over my rifle and my army uniform. I knew that never again would I be willing to pick up a gun at the command of a South African army officer.

Martin Luther King says:

> Wisdom born of experience should tell us that war is obsolete. There may have been a time when war served as a negative good by preventing the spread and growth of an evil force, but the destructive power of modern weapons eliminates even the possibility that war may serve as a negative good. If we assume that life is worth living and that man has a right to survival, then we must find an alternative to war.[57]

My own experience, and that of many, many others, tells me that killing people because the government tells you to is a terrible thing. How many wars do we have to fight before the human race finally learns how to put an end to war? How many more have to die, have to be crippled or maimed or have to live the remainder of their lives under the shadow of post-traumatic stress and depression? Can there be anything more utterly contrary to the spirit and teaching of Jesus than war?

Thomas Merton and the struggle against war

Thomas Merton is probably the most important and influential writer on contemplation and Christian spirituality of the past hundred years.

In his life as a Trappist monk, Merton gradually 'came to realise that contemplation of necessity summons one to action and social engagement', writes William H. Shannon. 'When he first became a monk, he saw the world only as something from which he wanted to escape.'[58]

Merton wanted to give himself completely to God, and as a young man he believed that this meant forsaking the world utterly. He wrote in 1948, 'That is the only reason why I desire solitude – to be lost to all created things, to die to them and to the knowledge of them, for they remind me of my distance from You.'[59]

But Merton's experience as a contemplative monk soon changed his understanding of what God required of him. Shannon says:

> Fourteen years later (October 1961) in the pages of *The Catholic Worker*, the same man is writing with passion and a sense of indignation that the one task God imposes on us in our day is to work for the total abolition of war. Christians, he says, must become active, with every ounce of concern, in leading the way toward a non-violent solution to international conflicts: They must mobilize all their resources for the struggle against war. Every other responsibility to which we are called is secondary in importance.[60]

The closer we come to Jesus Christ, the more we will recognise that war is a very great evil. A contemplative heart which is centred in the love of God in Christ will love peacemaking, gentleness, forgiveness and reconciliation. The heart which is ruled by the love of God will abhor violence and killing and war. We will long with every fibre of our being for an end to war. We will work and pray and speak out for the elimination of all nuclear weapons from the face of the earth.

There can be no possible sense in which the love of God for his world could ever see the destruction of a nuclear war as a good or right course of action for humankind. In November 2019 Pope Francis visited Nagasaki and Hiroshima and met with survivors of the 1945 atomic bombings. Speaking in Nagasaki, Pope Francis condemned the 'unspeakable horror' of nuclear weapons:

> In a world where millions of children and families live in inhumane conditions, the money that is squandered and the fortunes made through the manufacture, upgrading, maintenance and sale of ever more destructive weapons, are an affront crying out to heaven.[61]

Christians are always and in every circumstance called to be peace-makers: 'Blessed are the peacemakers, for they will be called children of God' (Matthew 5:9). It is difficult to see how peacemaking can ever involve or require the use of violence, though the nature of our world means that this may not be a simple or clear-cut matter.

My father was 20 years old in 1939, when World War II began. He spent six years fighting with the British Army in the Western Sahara, in the 7th Armoured Division (the Desert Rats). He never spoke much about what he had seen and experienced in those years, but I have no doubt that he was traumatised by what he had been through. I grew up with a father who was loving and caring but prone to frightening outbursts of anger. You could not argue with him or cross him. Something damaged and broken was locked up inside him, and we all suffered with him. This is what war does to people.

But was it right that my father, along with so many others, should give those six years of the prime of his life to fight against Hitler and Nazi Germany? What would have been the consequences had he and many, many others not made this sacrifice? What would have happened to the Jews? What would have become of civilisation in Europe and beyond? It seems to me that evil has to be confronted and stopped in its tracks. This is required of every generation in some way or other. For my father's generation it was necessary that a great evil should be opposed resolutely, and I believe that military force was required for that to happen. For peace to prevail, nations need to be able to defend themselves. A just war is sometimes therefore a possibility.

None of this means that followers of Jesus Christ should be in any doubt that the way of Jesus is the way of non-violence and peace-making. There is nothing good to be said about war. There is certainly nothing good about nuclear weapons. I have sometimes been out walking in the Yorkshire Dales, in one of the most beautiful and peaceful areas in Britain, when out of nowhere a jet fighter has thundered down the valley. Suddenly the peace is shattered, broken by the deafening wail of this vastly expensive war machine. Once I would have been interested to see a jet fighter flying overhead; now it speaks to me only of war and killing and the vast public expenditure that goes into arms manufacturing.

Making peace through the cross

Jesus Christ calls all those who would be his disciples to be instruments of his peace. At the very centre of the Christian faith is the cross of Christ. The cross is the place where God is most clearly visible to us. The love of God is revealed above all in the death of Jesus. Here we see God in human form, God the Son, participating in our sinful humanity and transforming it. In the cross we see God saying 'Yes' to our humanity – to our weakness, our struggles, our frailty and our pain.

The cross of Jesus is a symbol of peace, of the peace which God alone can bring us. The cross stands on a hill, as a symbol of irrelevance and failure. The world at that moment was saying, 'Jesus, you are irrelevant, and now you are finished. It's over.' But from the margins, from the place of weakness and being left behind, the cross of Jesus has found a way to speak powerfully into every human condition. Through the cross, God has proclaimed peace to those 'who were far off and peace to those who were near' (Ephesians 2:17).

For Christians, we come every Sunday to the cross and to the body and blood of Jesus, and find that somehow, in some mysterious way, this gives us hope and peace and courage. It is here that we find God reconciling us to himself and also reconciling us to one another, and we experience that transformation:

> But now in Christ Jesus you who once were far off have been brought near by the blood of Christ. For he is our peace; in his flesh he has made both groups into one and has broken down the dividing wall, that is, the hostility between us. He has abolished the law with its commandments and ordinances, so that he might create in himself one new humanity in place of the two, thus making peace, and might reconcile both groups to God in one body through the cross, thus putting to death that hostility through it.
> EPHESIANS 2:13–16

In the cross and in the blood of Christ we experience God reaching out to us, putting to death the hostility between us, making peace. We are then able to reach out to God and those around us. The cross above all is about love: that God so loved the world that he sent his Son to die for us. On the cross we see the full extent of the love of Jesus, who showed us how to live and who laid down his life for others.

The way of Jesus is the offering of kindness and generosity to all those who offend or hurt us. We love our enemies and pray for those who persecute us (Matthew 5:44). Jesus says, 'If anyone strikes you on the right cheek, turn the other also; and if anyone wants to sue you and take your coat, give your cloak as well; and if anyone forces you to go one mile, go also the second mile' (Matthew 5:39–41). We seek always to walk in the pattern of the Lord Jesus Christ, who, as he was being crucified, spoke these extraordinary words: 'Father, forgive them; for they do not know what they are doing' (Luke 23:34).

But Jesus also calls his disciples to be willing to challenge evil and hypocrisy and those who oppress the weak and the poor. Jesus was put to death on the cross because he refused to compromise with the oppression and suffering that surrounded him. Some of this was caused by disease, mental anguish and poverty, and some by the authorities, especially the priests and scribes, who placed impossible burdens on the shoulders of the poor. Jesus knew that his stance would lead him into conflict and trouble and ultimately to death, but he did not back down. He became a threat to those in authority, and that is why he was arrested and put to death.

In South Africa during the 1970s and 1980s the issue of conscription and military service became a serious problem for many young white South African men. As we realised more and more what it was that we were being called up to do, and why we were required to do this, many faced agonising decisions. It is never easy being a conscientious objector when many people in your own community believe that the policies of the government should be respected and obeyed. To refuse to serve in the armed forces for reasons of conscience and personal integrity is likely to lead to misunderstanding and persecution.

In 1971 the National Catholic Federation of Students issued a statement aimed particularly at supporting Christian students who were struggling with this issue. The statement declared that 'conscientious objection is totally in keeping with Christian principles and may even be demanded by them', and it went on to suggest that an alternative to military training should be offered by the South African government: 'Those choosing this could be required to give a similar period to that of military training building schools, hospitals, dams and other such constructions and working in underprivileged areas for the education and benefit of local communities.'[62]

One young Christian who chose to be a conscientious objector was Graham Philpott. Graham's father, Professor Hugh Philpott, was a head of department at the University of Natal Medical School and had been a missionary doctor in Nigeria. Hugh Philpott describes what happened to Graham in his autobiography, Learning for Life:

> Then there was the saga of Graham's military call-up. He agreed to enter the army as a Chaplain's assistant, on the understanding that he would be non-combatant. This was agreed to by the

army and he went to Voortrekkerhoogte to start his service. However, on the first massive parade for the new conscripts, they were told in graphic terms by the Commandant how they would be trained to annihilate the enemy (their fellow black South Africans!). Graham left the parade and went to the side of the parade ground, where a sergeant came to ask him if he was feeling unwell. When Graham told the sergeant that he was leaving the parade because he was unwilling to participate in what the Commandant was proposing, he was taken into detention. Some while later he was court martialled, but at the hearing he was able to defend his position and instead of military service he was able to do a period of community service with a priest working in Khayelitsha, a township near Cape Town. I am sure that this achieved more in the cause of peace than the military services required by the government of the day.[63]

This is an example of costly discipleship and obedience to Christ in the face of complex demands. It requires extraordinary courage to act as Graham Philpott acted on the parade ground at Voortrekkerhoogte. There are bound to be times and situations when anyone who is committed to following the teaching of Jesus Christ will have to leave the parade because they are not willing to participate in what is being asked of them. This is what peacemaking may require of us. We choose life, not death; peace, not war; love, not hatred; the way of Jesus, not the way of oppression and suffering.

14

Slowing down in the age of speed

It was Saturday morning and I was enjoying being in town. I had coffee with my wife and then I wandered around to our local bookshop. In the upstairs area amid the book tables and armchairs a man was loudly reciting a poem from memory. When he finished, I asked him who the poet was. He said G.K. Chesterton, and then asked me what my favourite poem was. I thought for a moment, then said 'Fern Hill' by Dylan Thomas. He found the poem in an anthology and asked me if I would read it aloud. I said, 'Yes, okay, but I'll only read the first verse, because it's quite long.' 'That's all right,' he said, 'we've got all day.' 'We've got all day?' I said. 'Yes, we have.' What a great thing to say, I thought.

Every one of us has got all day. This day is a gift that we have each been given. It is up to us to decide what we are going to do with it. We can rush around getting lots of things done. Or we can stop and read some poetry, and think about life and beauty and what it all might or might not mean. We've got all day.

Everywhere around us life seems to have been continually speeding up. It has been said that we live in the age of acceleration. Everything has been getting faster – computers, cars, news, food. We now expect to be able to do so much more in one day than our parents or grand-parents might have thought possible. Even pedestrians today move faster than they did in the 1990s, and the more developed the country, the quicker they walk. At the same time we are becoming more impatient. A third of people will now abandon websites that take more than two seconds to load. Twenty years ago they would have been willing to wait four times as long.[64]

It is hard for many of us to slow down, and almost impossible to stop and be still for a while. I am writing this as the coronavirus pandemic is taking hold of the world, and everything is changing around us. Right now, nobody knows how this is going to end and what the consequences are going to be. I am aware of a struggle within myself to adapt and slow down, while at the same time wanting to return as soon as possible to my former busy and active way of life. For now that is not possible. All of us are being forced, whether we like it or not, to let go of a lot of our former habits and expectations. Right now our greatest need is to be kind to one another, to stay safe, to pull together and to protect those at greatest risk. A change is happening, partly because none of us can have what we want right now. We simply have to be patient and wait. So maybe there are some important lessons that we can learn in the midst of a terrible disease that is sweeping across our planet.

I have no idea how all this is going to unfold. Maybe in a year or two most of us will have returned to the sped-up version of life that we had become so used to. But this seems to be an extraordinary moment to be reflecting upon the need for slowing down in an age of speed. It feels to me as though I have been driving for hours at 70 mph and then suddenly find myself on a dangerous, twisting and narrow road where it is not safe to go faster than 10 mph. For many of us, a radical shift in attitude is required if we are to accept a slower and quieter pace of life. This is all part of the struggle to return to a contemplative heart, a heart which is attuned to the heart of God. We may feel that there are a lot of things which are not getting done. But we also find ourselves having more time for other things, perhaps more time to think and to appreciate what we do have, and more time to be patient with others who are also struggling in these testing and troubled times.

There is a kind of madness in the speed-driven, frenetic way of living that has become the norm across much of the developed world. We try to do so much, and we can only manage this by pushing and rushing, by attending to some things and neglecting others. We prize efficiency and speed, being highly focused and mobile. We are perhaps more adept at this than any previous generation, but this is nothing new. Human beings have always had a weakness for speed, and the sense of power and exhilaration that it brings.

Returning and rest

We see something of this in Isaiah:

> For thus said the Lord God, the Holy One of Israel: In returning and rest you shall be saved; in quietness and in trust shall be your strength. But you refused and said, 'No! We will flee upon horses' – therefore you shall flee! and, 'We will ride upon swift steeds' – therefore your pursuers shall be swift!
> ISAIAH 30:15–16

When I read this passage it brings to mind the image of powerful cars speeding up and down the motorway, many going as fast as they can in the traffic, but always being followed by more and more cars, seemingly desperate to get somewhere as quickly as possible. Into this rat race, the Lord says, 'In returning and rest you shall be saved; in quietness and in trust shall be your strength.' In other words, the Lord says, 'Slow down. Come home and rest.' That is how you will be saved, not by this crazy charging around everywhere. It is in quietness and in learning to trust God in all circumstances that we will find the strength that we need for life's challenges. We depend upon God, and not ultimately on our own efforts to work things out.

John Ortberg writes about the spiritual discipline of 'slowing' in his book *The Life You've Always Wanted: Spiritual disciplines for ordinary people*. Ortberg defines slowing as 'cultivating patience by deliberately choosing to place ourselves in positions where we simply have to wait'.[65] Slowing down is all about learning to wait, especially for others, and to be gentle and patient. Instead of instant gratification and getting a result, we choose the way of quietness and trust. We depend upon God to provide our needs. It doesn't all depend on me.

My wife and I have over the past year largely given up on using motorways. We prefer to find the quieter roads, even if that means we may take longer to get to our destination. We try to take our time over things, to enjoy what we are doing and make the most of it, instead of rushing on to the next thing. It's a good phrase to remember: let's take our time. After all, we've got all day. The time is God's gift to us. Let's enjoy it and be thankful for it. As Psalm 118:24 says, 'This is the day that the Lord has made; let us rejoice and be glad in it.'

The heart of Jesus

When we take our time, and stop rushing from one thing to the next, we are learning to live in the present moment. This is what we see in the life of Jesus. He was always open and attentive to the person or people immediately in front of him, and able to respond with wisdom and compassion to each person's needs.

A good example is found in Mark 5:21–43. Jesus had been asked by Jairus, a leader of the synagogue, to come and heal his daughter, who was at the point of death. On the way to the house of Jairus, a woman in desperate need of healing came up behind Jesus and touched his cloak. He immediately stopped and turned around and listened to the woman who had touched him. 'Daughter, your faith has made you well; go in peace, and be healed of your disease,' he said (v. 34). Jesus then went on his way to see Jairus' daughter, and when he got there he raised her from the dead.

Jesus was never in a rush. He seems to have had all the time in the world. He was not pressured or stressed by other people's demands or expectations. He was able to be fully present to each person that he spent time with. Surely this was the direct result of Jesus' intimate relationship with the Father, which he maintained by spending time each day in prayer and solitude, usually very early in the morning. 'The Father and I are one,' said Jesus (John 10:30). Because of his oneness with the Father, Jesus was able to do everything according to the Father's perfect will and purpose for him: 'Very truly, I tell you, the Son can do nothing on his own, but only what he sees the Father doing' (John 5:19).

This is the key to the spiritual discipline of slowing: it is all about our hearts. If our hearts are aligned to God's heart of love, we will be able to live our lives according to his will, for us and for all his creation. This is what we see in Jesus. This is what Jesus is talking about when he tells us that we should abide in him as he abides in us (John 15:4). When the centre of our lives is in Christ, we are set free from what Paul calls 'the law of sin and of death' (Romans 8:2). The law of sin and death is the inexorable working out of our hearts being ruled and controlled by self rather than by God. The question for each of us is this: who or what is ruling my heart?

If our hearts, our deepest identities, are ruled by the 'me-first' self, by what the Bible calls the flesh, then we are living lives of sin. Sin is essentially putting what I want before what God wants. But the good news is that Christ has set us free from the slavery of being ruled by our self-centred human nature: 'There is therefore now no condemnation for those who are in Christ Jesus. For the law of the Spirit of life in Christ Jesus has set you free from the law of sin and of death' (Romans 8:1–2). When we turn to Jesus and make him our Lord and our Saviour, we are given a new heart, and a new Spirit is poured into our inmost being. The old, hard heart of stone is taken away and replaced with a new, soft heart, a heart of love that is a copy of God's own heart. This is beautifully expressed in Charles Wesley's hymn 'Oh, for a heart to praise my God':

O, for a heart to praise my God,
a heart from sin set free,
with conscience sprinkled by the blood
so freely shed for me.

A heart resigned, submissive, meek,
my great Redeemer's throne;

where only Christ is heard to speak,
where Jesus reigns alone.

A humble, lowly, contrite heart,
believing, true, and clean,
which neither life nor death can part
from him that dwells within.

A heart in every thought renewed,
and full of love divine;
perfect and right and pure and good –
a copy, Lord, of thine.

Thy nature, gracious Lord, impart,
come quickly from above;
write thy new name upon my heart,
thy new, best name of Love.[66]

This, surely, is the contemplative heart.

Much of this comes back to our abiding or dwelling in Christ. When our hearts are rooted and held firm in the love of Jesus, we are set free from the driven way of life of relentless pressure and endless demands. The nature of Jesus is in stark contrast to the way of our world as we often encounter it. The way of the world says, 'I'm in a hurry; get out of my way.' The way of Jesus says, 'Do not resist an evildoer. But if anyone strikes you on the right cheek, turn the other also' (Matthew 5:39). Instead of the competing, the pushing and the shoving, we respond to everyone with gentleness and compassion. Instead of riding roughshod over the weak, we take time to care for one another and to help those who are struggling along the way.

It's a tough world, and the reality of life is that we are all struggling in different ways. It will be a wonderful thing if in these days of crisis and change we can learn something more about being gentle and humble in heart, so that what matters most in any situation is that we care for one another, and that we are gentle and kind to one another. This will bring about a process of healing, where God's love will be at work to bring hope and a new care for one another and for the planet.

Jon M. Sweeney has written very helpfully about gentleness as a virtue which we desperately need now. These are his suggestions about the commitments we might make towards being gentle:

1 To commit myself daily to being truly present where I am: my place, my neighbourhood, among people with whom I live most closely.
2 To know the creatures around me, and look out for their welfare.
3 To live on earth more lightly and less violently in the food, products and energy I consume.
4 To draw strength and guidance from the Creation by listening more carefully to creatures of all kinds.
5 To walk and talk more quietly – to open and close doors more gently!
6 To respond to anger with gentleness, even when that means I may be perceived as 'weak'.
7 To touch people and things more carefully, and be aware of how my presence impacts others.
8 To listen with more careful attentiveness.
9 To pursue a daily practice of prayer, contemplation or worship that keeps my mind clear and my heart focused on these things.[67]

These are helpful and wise suggestions about how we might live in testing and troubled times. They offer us a picture of living from a contemplative heart, 'a humble, lowly, contrite heart', 'full of love divine'. This is the heart of love, the heart 'where only Christ is heard to speak, where Jesus reigns alone'.

If our desire is for such a heart as this, we can have confidence that God will answer our prayer as we ask each day, 'Thy nature, gracious Lord, impart, come quickly from above; write thy new name upon my heart, thy new, best name of Love.'

15

A people of hope

Hope offers the substance of all theology to the individual soul. By hope all the truths that are presented to the whole world in an abstract and impersonal way become for me a matter of personal and intimate conviction. What I believe by faith, what I understand by the habit of theology, I possess and make my own by hope. Hope is the gateway to contemplation, because contemplation is an experience of divine things and we cannot experience what we do not in some way possess. By hope we lay hands on the substance of what we believe and by hope we possess the substance of the promise of God's love.[68]

This is a wonderful piece of writing by Thomas Merton on the subject of hope. Hope is a notoriously difficult concept to pin down. Hope in the Christian sense of the word is something far greater than wishful thinking. This is not about saying that we hope the weather will be better tomorrow or that we hope we can make our flight connection at the airport. Christian hope is 'the substance of all theology to the individual soul', as Merton says. And also, says Merton, 'hope is the gateway to contemplation', and indeed to the Christian understanding of the contemplative life.

To followers of Christ, our hearts are rooted and grounded in a great and unchangeable hope. This is the hope which Paul expounds in the letter to the Romans, the hope by which we believe that neither 'height, nor depth, nor anything else in all creation, will be able to separate us from the love of God in Christ Jesus our Lord' (Romans 8:39). And so Paul prays, 'May the God of hope fill you with all joy and peace in believing, so that you may abound in hope by the power of the Holy Spirit' (Romans 15:13).

Thomas Merton is saying much the same as Paul. It is in believing, in 'what I believe by faith', as Merton says, that we may come to abound in hope. We are then filled with all joy and peace in our hearts by the God of hope. God is the source of our hope, not any earthly circumstances or events. In fact, this hope is completely independent of earthly events and the situations in which we find ourselves. As the first letter of Peter says, 'Blessed be the God and Father of our Lord Jesus Christ! By his great mercy he has given us new birth into a living hope through the resurrection of Jesus Christ from the dead' (1 Peter 1:3). Our hope as Christians is bound entirely to the person of Jesus Christ and to his resurrection from the dead.

Hope is personal. Hope transforms my inner being and my sense of what my life is about. Hope is the gateway to contemplation, says Merton. The contemplation that Merton is talking about here is not mindfulness or meditation as it is widely taught these days. This is much more than a daily discipline of sitting silently and paying attention to our thoughts and our breathing. Mindfulness commonly involves a practice of staying in the present moment for a short period of time as a way of releasing stress and anxiety. There is certainly much value in this, but Merton has something very different in mind.

Contemplation, says Merton, 'is an experience of divine things'. This is why hope is the gateway to contemplation, because 'by hope we possess the substance of the promise of God's love'. This quote is taken from Merton's book *No Man Is an Island*, from a chapter entitled 'Sentences in hope'. Merton goes on, in the next paragraph, to be specific about how we may know the promise of God's love. He says, 'Jesus is the theology of the Father. If I do not hope in His love for me, I will never really know Christ.'[69] Contemplation in the Christian tradition is centred on Christ. For Merton, what I believe by faith in Jesus, and then make my own by hope, is essential to contemplative practice.

This understanding of hope is very significant for us who are now living in the third decade of the 21st century. We are living in wild and strange days. Our consciousness is daily buffeted by news of poverty and inequality, the climate emergency, racism, disease, war and violence. We live in a digital world, in the age of acceleration, and none of us is in control of what is happening to our lives. We all know that we are not capable of dealing with the challenges that are ranged against us. The weight of the world is heavy upon many shoulders and hearts, and for many, signs of hope are hard to find. As we think about the world that our children and grandchildren may be facing, we may well be filled with anxiety and even despair.

So a huge question for our time is this: where do we find hope? To answer this for myself, I am drawn back again to my own experience in South Africa in the 1970s. When I joined UCM, we shared a vision of a just and free South Africa. Within five years, UCM had been crushed by the apartheid government. Its leaders were either banned or driven into exile. I and many others who had joined UCM were shaken to the core by what had happened. In those days it was very tough to think that the kind of change for which we longed and prayed would ever come to South Africa.

In these circumstances, it was all too easy to give up or to give in. Yet in South Africa I and many others were able to find hope through faith in Christ, and through our experience of Christian communities and churches. Hope does not ultimately come from looking at a desperate situation and trying to plan a way forward. This may help, and it may be an important thing to do, but sometimes we face forces that are just too powerful and our situation may, humanly speaking, seem hopeless. At that time in South Africa, I was privileged to know and work with those who showed me the way of Christ by their faith and by their example. This is what made all the difference to me and to many others in those days of struggle. Through our hope in God, we found the strength to persevere, to continue to work for justice and to keep on believing that a new South Africa would one day be born.

I am often drawn to Psalm 121:1–2, where the psalmist says, 'I lift up my eyes to the hills – from where will my help come? My help comes from the Lord, who made heaven and earth.' There, in a few simple words, is the answer to our cry. Where do we find hope in a broken and suffering world? Our help comes from the Lord, the maker of all things in heaven and earth.

Merton is right to say that hope is the gateway to contemplation. But I would also want to say that it is our practice of contemplative prayer that grounds us in hope. As this practice becomes established in our daily lives, we will find that increasingly we draw our hope from the still centre. This is the place where the love of God rules in our inmost being, where we simply *know* that his love is the final word in all our human experience. Here, in the place of daily letting go and self-emptying, we learn to abide and rest and trust in God, no matter what is going on around us. This is where our hope is nurtured and sustained. This is where we know, like Paul, that nothing in all creation 'will be able to separate us from the love of God in Christ Jesus our Lord' (Romans 8:39).

Knowing the peace which the world cannot give

In times such as these many people are living daily with fear and anxiety, and perhaps even a sense of despair. As the effects of climate change become more and more apparent, and as authoritarian leaders become more and more powerful, we are all vulnerable to fear and anxiety.

A daily practice of contemplative silent prayer can enable our hearts to be held firm in God's love and in the peace which passes under-standing. In addition to this, there is a prayer which I have found immensely helpful as a means to secure my own heart in rest and quietness and trust, no matter what is happening around me:

> O God, from whom all holy desires, all good counsels, and all just works do proceed: Give unto thy servants that peace which the world cannot give; that both our hearts may be set to obey thy

commandments, and also that by thee we being defended from
the fear of our enemies may pass our time in rest and quietness;
through the merits of Jesus Christ our Saviour. Amen

The Collect for Peace[70]

This prayer will be familiar to all those who know the old Anglican
prayer book service of evening prayer. It is a prayer which I now use
every day, because it expresses some of the deepest longings of my
own heart.

We begin with God. We are reminded that the God to whom we come
at the close of the day is a good and holy and just God. We can trust
him with our lives, because of who he is. He knows how my day has
gone, what has gone well and what has gone badly. We return at the
close of each day to the unchanging eternal reality of almighty God,
the creator and sustainer of all that is.

He is the one who is the source of all our holy longings and desires.
He is the God of truth and wisdom, the giver of all good counsels. All
the just and righteous works that we have been enabled to do have
flowed from his hand and from his Spirit within us. He is the God of
holiness, the God of wisdom and the God of justice.

To be made holy means that all our desires increasingly become holy.
We want what God wants. We love what God loves. This is the contemplative heart. Those things that are not good and true and lovely in
God's eyes become distasteful to us. The more we love God, the more
we will want him to rule our heart and to direct our desires. So in
this prayer at the close of each day, we acknowledge our dependence
upon God's good counsels and his holy wisdom to direct our hearts
and lives.

The prayer also reminds us that 'the Lord is a God of justice' (Isaiah
30:18) and the source of all just works. His justice is true and complete,
without any partiality or prejudice. He favours no one above anyone
else. He is a God who cares passionately for those who suffer because

of injustice, for the poor, the exploited and the suffering. We see this over and over again in the Bible, especially in the Old Testament prophets and in the life and teaching of Jesus. We should have no doubt whatsoever about whose side God is on when we see justice denied and the poor exploited and oppressed.

This prayer takes us, first, to God as the anchor of our being and of our world. His unchanging nature and truth are where we need to go, first of all, at the end of each day. So we bring our hearts to God and we ask that he may give us his peace, which the world cannot give. We ask this not only because we need relief from the stress of our daily lives; we ask for the peace which the world cannot give in order that our hearts may be set free to obey God's commandments.

The peace that God gives us in Christ is not the same as the peace the world knows and understands. This is an interior peace, which is not dependent on our circumstances, nor is it diminished or impaired by how tired we are or how discouraged, distracted or dismayed we may be. This is the peace that passes all human understanding.

The fruit of this peace is that our hearts are set to obey Christ's commandments. Above all this means that our hearts are ruled by the love of Jesus. The more the Spirit of Christ rules in our hearts, the more we will be set free from self-seeking and self-interest, in order to obey Jesus and to live a life of love. 'This is my commandment, that you love one another as I have loved you,' says Jesus to his disciples (John 15:12).

Then, second, the fruit of this peace is that our hearts are released from fear and anxiety. This is what Jesus promised: 'Peace I leave with you; my peace I give to you. I do not give to you as the world gives. Do not let your hearts be troubled, and do not let them be afraid' (John 14:27). We are defended by God from the fear of our enemies, because 'perfect love casts out fear' (1 John 4:18).

We are held by love and defended from fear by the peace of God within us. This deep inner peace holds us firm and fast through all the storms and turbulence of daily life. It is the still centre, the interior silence, which will enable us to pass our time in rest and quietness. This is not likely to be a life without struggle or difficulty; this is rather a life where our interior reality is rest and quietness, even amid crises and emergencies, illnesses and tragedies. Through our trust in God, and our daily returning to his mercy and grace, we are kept safe within our hearts by his peace. To come back again to Isaiah: 'For thus said the Lord God, the Holy One of Israel: In returning and rest you shall be saved; in quietness and in trust shall be your strength' (30:15).

The Collect for Peace is a prayer that we can use at the close of each day to come back to the contemplative heart. The God to whom we are praying is a God whose nature is holiness, justice and wisdom. This is the God in whom we are putting our trust in all the struggles we face. Our God is committed to the triumph of justice and righteousness, wisdom and truth, holiness and goodness. This is his very nature. When we stand up for these things, we do not stand alone. We stand with God, and we trust that his purposes will ultimately triumph. This is why Desmond Tutu could say, 'For we who are Christians, the death and resurrection of Jesus Christ are proof positive that love is stronger than hate, that life is stronger than death, that light is stronger than darkness.'[71] Victory is ours through him who loves us (see Romans 8:37, NLT).

Conclusion

As I write this, it is the year 2020, and we are living through a time when the coronavirus is changing everything. A new world is being born. No one knows what this will mean or what this new world will look like. But one thing seems sure: we will never go back to everything being just as it was BC – before coronavirus.

We are living in strange and wild times. Established habits of life are being tested and many are being found wanting. The old is passing away and soon the new post-coronavirus world will emerge. Could these be the days of the great correction, the great turning back to a more humane and just future for our world? Certainly many of us have been longing for such a turning, and have been aware that it was not likely to happen unless somehow or other we were all stopped in our tracks. Covid-19 is a terrible disease, bringing untold suffering to millions of people. But it has brought us to a point of having to stop, to ask some big and important questions and to start learning to live in ways which would have been unthinkable just a few months ago.

In the times that lie ahead, beyond Covid-19 and this pandemic, I believe we will need to look to the kind of world that awaits us in the coming decades of the 21st century. Already we see giants looming up out of the fog: the climate emergency, poverty and disease, nuclear weapons, nationalism and populism. Many young people, and some older people, believe that we can change the world for the better. We believe that we should be able to face the challenge of climate change and learn to care for our planet. We want a world where everyone receives decent and fair wages, where everyone has access to good healthcare and education and a clean environment. We want a world that is free of nuclear weapons.

My hope and prayer are that, as we head into these uncharted waters, we will have a clearer sense of what is truly important. As a result of this pandemic we have an opportunity to recalibrate, perhaps even to start afresh. Much is being pruned away. This is a great refining, such as the world has not known for over half a century. Many of us have lived through a time of excess, of unparalleled indulgence, with the world as our playground. We have behaved like huge, spoilt children, heedless of the mayhem and the consequences that our behaviour has left behind. Now we all know that we are not in control. We cannot treat the natural world as our servant forever. There are things out there that are too big even for the largest banks and multinationals.

It seems to me that we are being pulled back to a slower pace of life, to the contemplative heart, and I believe this is where the hope for our future lies. It begins not with regaining control and carrying on as before. Instead we have, first of all, to come back to our own hearts, our own true and deepest selves. We have to rediscover who we are and what we have been created for. We are not here on earth simply to enjoy and indulge ourselves. The invitation that the 21st century now offers to each of us is this: will you return to your true self and make your own unique contribution to the saving and healing of our world?

So this is a time to step back from our busy, driven ways of living and to reconnect with our creator God, with the people who matter to us, especially our families and friends, and to learn again to listen. This time brings to each of us an invitation from God to enter into a new pattern of life – to go deeper and to live more simply and quietly and generously.

The contemplative way begins with stopping, with solitude and being still, with waiting and hoping and trusting. In the resurrection of Jesus Christ from the dead we have the ultimate declaration of the victory of divine love over all the powers of darkness and despair. We are the Easter people; we believe in the power of the resurrection of our Lord Jesus Christ. This is what gives us hope and saves us from despair.

Without faith, without this great hope in Christ, we have only ourselves to turn to. We can look to science, to technology or to capitalism, but none of these has the power to save us from ourselves and from our own greed and self-interest. It is faith that changes everything, and it is faith in Christ and his resurrection that reveals to us the unconquerable power of love. The love of God in Christ Jesus is the final word upon which all our futures depend.

When our hearts are aligned with the heart of God and his everlasting love, we will find the way to live in the world that lies before us now. We may be asking: what is God's will for my life, now and in the days to come? It's simple. God's purpose for me – and, I believe, for each one of us – is to live a life of love, kindness, goodness, patience, truthfulness, generosity, gentleness and mercy. If we all do this, then surely a new day will dawn for the healing of the nations. Then we will see 'justice roll down like waters, and righteousness like an ever-flowing stream' (Amos 5:24).

What does the Lord require of you
but to do justice, and to love kindness,
*   and to walk humbly with your God?*
MICAH 6:8

Appendix

Contemplative practice[72]

Theophan the Recluse was a Russian Orthodox monk who died in 1894. He wrote a number of books on the Christian life, prayer and spirituality. In his teaching on prayer, Theophan writes, 'I will remind you of only one thing: one must descend with the mind into the heart, and there stand before the face of the Lord, ever present, all seeing within you.'[73]

Theophan is describing the way in which we can learn to practise the presence of God in all the tasks and activities of our daily lives. As the prayer of the heart becomes part of who we are, we find that we are increasingly able to 'pray without ceasing', as the apostle Paul says in 1 Thessalonians 5:17. This is not a matter of saying prayers constantly but of being continually held in the presence of God. Contemplation, and contemplative practice, is chiefly concerned with opening the heart to the love of God in Christ. Understanding with our minds is important, but in a relationship it is the giving of the heart in love that is essential.

'I give you my heart,' we say to the one we love. When we truly love someone, we hopefully will think carefully about what we are doing. We will act with understanding and thoughtfulness. But love, freely and fully given, is not a calculation or a judgement. Love is a response from deep within us to someone or something that we care about. Love is a giving of ourselves which flows from the heart, from our inmost being, and is known to be genuine only when it is revealed in actions of compassion and self-sacrifice. When we give our hearts, we give ourselves. We lay down our lives for one another.

To learn contemplative practice is to engage ourselves every day in an unconditional opening of our hearts, our deepest and truest selves, to the God whose name is Love. He is the God and Father of our Lord Jesus Christ; he so loved the world that he gave his only Son in order that all those who put their trust in him will not perish but have everlasting life (John 3:16). 'We love because he first loved us' (1 John 4:19), and so perhaps the deepest and truest form of prayer is contemplation, the offering of our own hearts and our deepest selves in love to God, who first loved us.

How do we do this? In the Christian tradition there are a number of methods of contemplative prayer, the prayer of the heart, which are widely used and recognised. In the eastern monastic tradition, the practice of simply calling upon the name of the Lord Jesus Christ was considered to be most important, as the sacramental power of the name of Jesus is believed to open the heart to the indwelling power of the Holy Spirit. The Jesus Prayer, 'Lord Jesus Christ, Son of God, have mercy on me, a sinner', has in recent years spread into the lives and practice of many western Christians.

Lectio divina (divine reading) is a form of contemplative prayer in which we read a short passage of the Bible, and then slowly and quietly allow God to meet us and to speak to us through his word. There are four steps in this process. We start with *lectio* (reading), and then after a time of quiet we move to *meditatio* (meditation), then more silence, then *oratio* (prayer), and then finally *contemplatio* (contemplation). We read the passage carefully at the beginning of each stage, and we open our hearts to God in the silence that follows.

Christian meditation is 'a widely used method which involves the repetition of a single word faithfully and lovingly during the time of meditation'.[74] This again is an ancient Christian way of prayer that was recovered for modern Christians by the Benedictine monk, John Main (1926–82). In this method the emphasis is on becoming still through concentration on a word (or mantra) which is repeated faithfully, lovingly and continually.

Centring Prayer is another contemporary method of silent prayer which has become widely taught and used by millions around the world. Centring prayer was developed by Thomas Keating, a Cistercian (Trappist) monk from St Benedict's monastery in Colorado. His book *Open Mind, Open Heart* has sold over half a million copies in English and has been translated into a number of foreign-language editions. Here the emphasis is on surrender and letting go, rather than con-centration. I personally have found that the guidelines for Centring Prayer have helped me enormously in keeping a daily practice of silent prayer. The guidelines are very simple:

1 Choose a sacred word as the symbol of your intention to consent to God's presence and action within. The sacred word is chosen during a brief period of prayer to the Holy Spirit. We may use a word such as God, Jesus, Abba, Love, Peace or Trust. The sacred word is sacred not because of its inherent meaning, but because of the meaning we give it as the expression of our intention to consent.
2 Sitting comfortably and with eyes closed, settle briefly and silently introduce the sacred word as the symbol of your consent to God's presence and action within.
3 When engaged with your thoughts, return ever-so-gently to the sacred word.
4 At the end of the prayer period, remain in silence with eyes closed for a couple of minutes.[75]

This method of prayer is about simply being with God. Normally we would aim for a period of 20 minutes to be still in the presence of God, with a 'naked intent direct to God', as described in the 14th-century spiritual classic *The Cloud of Unknowing*.[76] This is our intention, the intention of our hearts before God. Of course, we will find ourselves aware of distractions and trains of thought that draw us away from this. Such 'thoughts are an inevitable, integral and normal part of Centering Prayer'.[77] Gently, as a feather on the breath of God, we return to the sacred word, to the still centre. There is no condemnation, no judgement, no such thing as a 'bad' time of Centring Prayer, or indeed, a 'good' time of Centring Prayer. The important thing is just turning up, just doing it. It is about simply *being* in the presence of God.

The practice of contemplative prayer is not complicated or difficult. But that is not to say that it is easy. It may sound straightforward to suggest that all we need to do is sit still in the presence of God for 20 minutes each day. But most if not all of us know that we can find all kinds of ways and reasons not to do this, and not to keep this time as a regular daily practice. Maybe we are too busy; maybe this kind of prayer seems to be a waste of our time. What is the point of just doing nothing for 20 minutes? That, in a way, is exactly the point. By doing nothing we are giving our whole attention to God. We are offering God our whole being without any agenda of our own. We empty ourselves, following the model of Jesus (see Philippians 2:5–7). We let go of all self-interest and self-concern, and we open our hearts to the one who loves us with a love that is as deep as the ocean, as vast as the open sky.

The truth is that some form of daily contemplative practice is essential if our hearts are to be deeply open to the Holy Spirit. If we are to be enabled to live in the freedom of Jesus, and to know our hearts radically transformed by his heart of love, we must spend time daily in a loving attentiveness to his holy presence. There is no other way.

Our lives may be full and busy, but that is all the more reason why it is important for us to have a daily discipline which helps us to maintain a measure of interior silence. We need this point of reference, this returning to the centre, in order to be attentive to God in all that we are doing. If our desire is that our lives should be pleasing to God in every way, we will be greatly strengthened by this practice. If we long to do God's will and to give ourselves fully to his service, we must find time in our daily routine for silence.

It is important to say that a contemplative response is not a withdrawal from the world or an opting out of the demands, busyness and stress of modern life. It is in fact the only way to remain true to Christ and to our own hearts as we engage in serving him in a complex and demanding world. Perhaps our greatest need is to be able, in the midst of all our work, to know an abiding sense of God's peace and presence and to be able to call upon him for help.

There is a short contemplative prayer based on Psalm 40:13 which can be used for this purpose many times during the day and the night: 'O God, make speed to save us. O Lord, make haste to help us.' The Christian monk and theologian John Cassian (c. 360–435) describes this prayer as the formula for contemplation which 'was given us by a few of the oldest Fathers who remained. To maintain an unceasing recollection of God it is to be ever set before you'. He goes on to say:

> This verse has been rightly selected from the whole Bible for this purpose. It fits every mood and temper of human nature, every temptation, every circumstance. It contains an invocation of God, a humble confession of faith, a reverent watchfulness, a meditation upon our frailty, confidence in God's answer, an assurance of his ever-present support.[78]

Our goal in all of this is to please God in everything we do. 'We keep before our minds the aim of pleasing him,' says St Basil (c. 329–379), another of the early church Fathers. He says:

> Thus in the midst of our work we can fulfil the duty of prayer, giving thanks to him who has granted strength to our hands for performing our tasks, and cleverness to our minds for acquiring knowledge… thus we acquire a recollected spirit, when in every action we beg from God the success of our labours and satisfy our debt of gratitude to him… and when we keep before our minds the aim of pleasing him.[79]

Contemplative practice is not primarily about a particular method or system. It is rather an attitude of the heart, which is expressed in a way of life and in a daily discipline which holds us in attentiveness to the love of God. Each of us will need to find our own way, our own practice, which enables us to live faithfully before God, and to be true to ourselves and to our own desire to serve and honour him. We find our own practice, and we seek the grace of God to keep this practice and to maintain this wherever possible.

Because this is a matter of the heart, where our deepest desires are involved, we will need to be accountable to others, to fellow-pilgrims who are trustworthy and who care for us. We need wise companions and those who are skilled in the art of discernment. The key in the development of the practice is the ability to recognise God's grace and his unfolding will and purpose for us. We need someone who can help us to be truthful with ourselves and with our motives and behaviour.

This is where finding a spiritual director or soul friend is so important. Then we will be able to come to a person who is 'on our side', who can help us to see what the Holy Spirit is up to in our lives. A good spiritual director will have experience from their own life and from the lives of those around them of seeing God at work, and of knowing that God is to be trusted completely in all his ways. Thus we can be guided, supported and given the encouragement and assurance that we need as we journey with God into a deeper integrity and obedience before him.

There are potentially many pitfalls and sources of discouragement and difficulty. Our false self will not easily allow us to 'let go' and empty ourselves before God. Contemplative practice is not about how I feel or what results I am seeing. It is not a win-lose, achievement-based activity. We are not seeking supernatural signs or mystical experiences. We are not seeking anything except the surrender of our hearts and lives to God. The real fruit of this will be the fruit of the Holy Spirit: love, joy, peace, patience, kindness, generosity, faithfulness, gentleness and self-control (Galatians 5:22–23). The measure of our practice will be our growth into the likeness and character of Jesus. Our practice must lead us to a greater love and service of others if it is genuinely centred on Jesus and not on our own experience and self-interest. This is not about my reward or my spiritual experiences, but about yielding to the Holy Spirit. This is all that matters in contemplative prayer.

In contemplation, we throw ourselves upon God in radical faith and dependence on him. We trust God in the darkness, where we have let go of our own desires for control, status and security. There are likely to be times when we feel deeply uncomfortable, and we may cling to any reason not to enter this arena. We may say that we have theological problems about this form of prayer, or we may say that it just doesn't work for me. Many people in our society are uncomfortable with any form of extended silence. It takes courage to sit still in the midst of all the storms of life, to let go of trying to think about the solutions and the issues, to wait and do nothing and let God be God in our hearts.

The way through is faith. If God is God, and his ways are not our ways, then we can surely, for a short period in each day, stop and place everything unconditionally in his hands. Contemplation is all about the life of faith, about depending wholly on God for all our needs, for everything. We allow the Holy Spirit to pray in us, in prayer that is beyond words, in our own weakness and helplessness before God (see Romans 8:26–27).

So in contemplative practice we train ourselves to live from the heart, not the head. We give our hearts to God in love. We allow the Holy Spirit to pray for us and in us, with sighs too deep for words. We cry 'Abba, Father!' Through this prayer and this practice, we learn day by day to trust and depend on God for everything.

Notes

1   Steve Biko, *I Write What I Like* (Penguin, 1988), p. 10.
2   Biko, *I Write What I Like*, p. 10.
3   Ronald J. Sider, 'Foreword' in Christopher Sugden, *Radical Discipleship* (Marshalls Paperbacks, 1981), p. iv.
4   Denise M. Ackermann, from a talk given at the 20-year celebration of the Centre, Stellenbosch, August 2007.
5   Ackermann, talk given at the 20-year celebration of the Centre.
6   Ackermann, talk given at the 20-year celebration of the Centre.
7   L.P. Hartley, *The Go-Between* (first published 1953).
8   Michael Parks, 'Tutu defuses tense funeral confrontation', *Los Angeles Times*, 7 August 1985, **latimes.com/archives/la-xpm-1985-08-07-mn-3691-story.html**.
9   Freedom '71 UCM publicity leaflet.
10 'Over to you…', University Christian Movement of Southern Africa leaflet.
11 SASO 1972 document quoted in Baruch Hirson, *Year of Fire, Year of Ash*, revised edition (Zed Books, 2016).
12 'Linkse broeines nou ontbloot', *Die Afrikaner*, 17 July 1970, p. 1.
13 Martin Luther King, *Strength to Love* (Collins/Fontana Books, 1970), p. 65.
14 Freedom '71 Conference Report, University Christian Movement 1971, p. 42.
15 William J. Houston, *A Critical Evaluation of the University Christian Movement as an Ecumenical Mission to Students, 1967–1972* (UNISA, 1997).
16 Houston, *A Critical Evaluation of the University Christian Movement as an Ecumenical Mission to Students, 1967–1972*.
17 John Morrison, 'The myth is dead', *NUX*, 10 June 1971.
18 'No trust and respect: Hurley', *NUX*, 31 August 1971.
19 Bishop Alpheus Zulu quoted in Hirson, *Year of Fire, Year of Ash*, p. 82.
20 'No trust and respect: Hurley'.
21 Anon., 'Sunday', *NUSAS Newsletter*, vol. 2, no. 41, October 1971.
22 Letter from Charles Parry, reproduced with permission.
23 Ian Cowley, 'Christian revival in South Africa', *NUX*, 5 April 1973.

24   Richard Rolle, *The Fire of Love* (Penguin Classics, 1972), back cover.
25   Rolle, *The Fire of Love*, pp. 120–21.
26   Rolle, *The Fire of Love*, p. 111.
27   Ian M. Macqueen, *Black Consciousness and Progressive Movements under Apartheid* (UKNZ Press, 2018), p. 47.
28   Richard Turner, *The Eye of the Needle* (Seagull Books, 2015), pp. 22–23.
29   Turner, *The Eye of the Needle*, pp. 26–27, 44.
30   'Honorary doctorates for outstanding contributions', *UKZNTouch* 2016, p. 63.
31   'Honorary doctorates for outstanding contributions', p. 64.
32   **kxc.org.uk/war-of-desires**
33   Alan Richardson (ed.), *A Theological Word Book of the Bible* (SCM, 1957), pp. 83–84.
34   Richardson (ed.), *A Theological Word Book of the Bible*, pp. 83–84.
35   Thomas Merton, *New Seeds of Contemplation* (New Directions, 1961), p. 32.
36   Merton, *New Seeds of Contemplation*, p. 25.
37   Rowan Williams, *Holy Living: The Christian tradition for today* (Bloomsbury, 2017), pp. 96–97.
38   'Where are we going?', *NUX*, 10 June 1971.
39   'Pollution: what you can do', *NUX*, 10 June 1971.
40   Biko, *I Write What I Like*, p. 82.
41   Biko, *I Write What I Like*, p. 104.
42   Biko, *I Write What I Like*, p. 114.
43   Biko, *I Write What I Like*, p. 114.
44   Macqueen, *Black Consciousness and Progressive Movements under Apartheid*, p. 235.
45   Macqueen, *Black Consciousness and Progressive Movements under Apartheid*, p. 211.
46   Macqueen, *Black Consciousness and Progressive Movements under Apartheid*, p. 212.
47   Quarterly Labour Force Survey: quarter 1, 2019.
48   'This is how much South Africans pay their domestic worker in 2019', *Businesstech*, 20 May 2019, **businesstech.co.za/news/ finance/317882/this-is-how-much-south-africans-pay-their-domestic-worker-in-2019**.
49   'The need to contribute', *NUX*, 7 October 1971, p. 2.
50   'The need to contribute'.
51   Charlie Manicom, *NUX*, 19 August 1971, p. 11.

52   For a full account of this time, see Ian Cowley, *A People of Hope* (Highland Books, 1993).

53   Louise Rose, Rebecca Winfrey and Claire Beaton, 'Rector's update', St George's Church Stamford, February 2020, p. 1.

54   Rose, Winfrey and Beaton, 'Rector's update', pp. 1–2.

55   Rose, Winfrey and Beaton, 'Rector's update', p. 2.

56   Cowley, *A People of Hope*, pp. 184–85,

57   Martin Luther King, *Strength to Love* (Collins/Fontana Books, 1970), p. 41.

58   William H. Shannon, *Thomas Merton's Paradise Journey* (Burns and Oates, 2000).

59   Thomas Merton, *The Seven Storey Mountain* (Harcourt Brace, 1948), p. 471.

60   Shannon, *Thomas Merton's Paradise Journey*, p. 247.

61   Justin McCurry, 'Pope Francis calls for a "world without nuclear weapons" during Nagasaki visit', *The Guardian*, 23 November 2019.

62   *NUX*, 16 September 1971.

63   Hugh Philpott, *Learning for Life: Lessons learned along the way* (Self-published, 2016), p. 191.

64   Tom Whipple, 'Don't stop me now: life is getting faster... and we like it that way', *The Times*, 25 March 2016.

65   John Ortberg, *The Life You've Always Wanted: Spiritual disciplines for ordinary people* (Zondervan, 2002), p. 83.

66   Charles Wesley, 'Oh, for a heart to praise my God' from *Hymns Ancient and Modern*, revised edition (William Clowes and Sons, 1950), no. 325, p. 258.

67   Jon M. Sweeney, 'Gentleness: A virtue we most desperately need now', *Fairacres Chronicle*, Summer 2018, p. 36.

68   Thomas Merton, *No Man Is an Island* (Burns and Oates, 1955), p. 19.

69   Merton, *No Man Is an Island*, p. 19.

70   The second collect at evening prayer, *The Book of Common Prayer* (Cambridge University Press).

71   Desmond Tutu, *No Future without Forgiveness* (Rider Books, 1999), p. 76.

72   This is an edited extract of Ian Cowley, 'Contemplation: The way to communion with God', *The Contemplative Response* (BRF, 2019), pp. 100–107.

73   Theophan the Recluse, quoted in Jean Khoury, 'Bringing the mind into the heart', Spirituality blog, 7 June 2014, **amorvincit.blogspot. com/2014/06/spirituality-108-bringing-mind-into.html**.

74 The World Community for Christian Meditation, 'Christian meditation in the UK', **christianmeditation.org.uk**.

75 Thomas Keating, *Open Mind, Open Heart*, 20th anniversary edition (Continuum, 2006), pp. 177–78. See also, Keating, 'The method of Centering Prayer', **contemplativeoutreach.org/wp-content/uploads/2012/04/method_cp_eng-2016-06_0.pdf**.

76 William Johnston (ed.), *The Cloud of Unknowing* (HarperCollins Fount, 1997), p. 22.

77 Keating, 'The method of Centering Prayer'.

78 John Cassian, *The Fire and the Cloud*, edited by David A. Fleming (Geoffrey Chapman, 1978), pp. 34–35.

79 Quoted in Thomas Merton, *Contemplative Prayer* (DLT, 2005), p. 35.

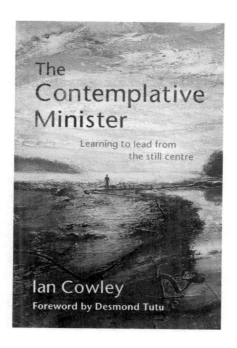

At one time Christian ministry offered the opportunity to spend your life in the study of God's word, in reading and reflection, in prayer and sermon preparation, and in the faithful pastoral care of a community. These days there are very few jobs in full-time ministry which do not require a heroic combination of stamina, multi-tasking and change management. Drawing on his experience of developing and leading relevant training programmes, Ian Cowley assesses the stresses and pressures of the job and shows how to grow into a 'contemplative minister', prioritising a relationship of deepening love with God.

The Contemplative Minister

Learning to lead from the still centre
Ian Cowley, with a foreword by Desmond Tutu
978 0 85746 360 9 £8.99

brfonline.org.uk

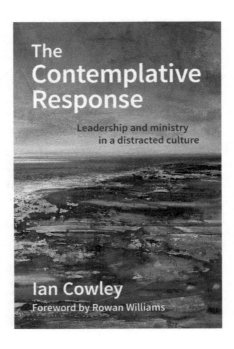

Following on from the success of *The Contemplative Minister*, Ian Cowley offers new insight and greater depth for church leaders in a distracted world. Ian emphasises that the true self finds peace in resting in the love of God. He addresses the compulsions of our consumerist culture and calls those in leadership to an inner life of truthfulness, self-knowledge and self-discipline.

The Contemplative Response
Leadership and ministry in a distracted culture
Ian Cowley, with a foreword by Rowan Williams
978 0 85746 656 3 £8.99

brfonline.org.uk

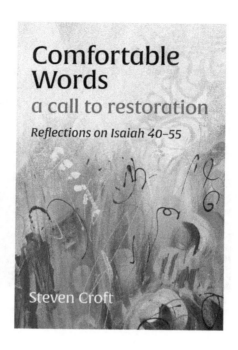

Comfortable Words
a call to restoration

Reflections on Isaiah 40–55

Steven Croft

Through nine reflections, Steven Croft examines what these 'comfortable words' have to say to us. Each reflection begins from a passage of scripture taken from Isaiah 40—55, the song of an unnamed prophet who sings at the end of the exile to call God's people home. The prophet sings of love and forgiveness and of new hope and strength in God, to rekindle courage in the hearts of God's people. These are comfortable words the whole world needs to hear afresh in this season.

Comfortable Words
Reflections on Isaiah 40—55
Steven Croft
978 1 80039 1 055 £7.99

brfonline.org.uk

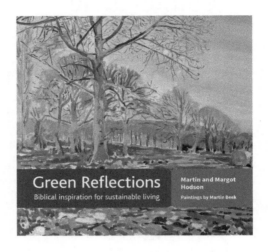

Martin and Margot Hodson offer 62 reflections inspired by passages from the Bible in this beautifully illustrated gift book encouraging reflection on and care for our environment.

Green Reflections
Biblical inspiration for sustainable living
Martin and Margot Hodson, with paintings by Martin Beek
978 1 80039 068 3 £8.99

brfonline.org.uk

Environmental sustainability is a major issue for us all. In this extensively updated edition, Martin and Margot Hodson consider eight of the key current environmental problems, giving the biblical basis for looking after the environment and helping to integrate environmental thinking into the reader's understanding of Christian faith. This accessible guide includes ethical reflections, Bible studies focusing on a different biblical doctrine for each chapter and eco-tips to enable practical response.

A Christian Guide to Environmental Issues
Fully revised and updated second edition
Martin J. Hodson and Margot R. Hodson
978 1 80039 005 8 £9.99

brfonline.org.uk

Enabling all ages to grow in faith

Anna Chaplaincy
Living Faith
Messy Church
Parenting for Faith

The Bible Reading Fellowship (BRF) is a Christian charity that resources individuals and churches. Our vision is to enable people of all ages to grow in faith and understanding of the Bible and to see more people equipped to exercise their gifts in leadership and ministry.

To find out more about our ministries, visit
brf.org.uk